BOUNCING BACK

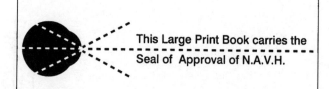

This Large Print Book carries the
Seal of Approval of N.A.V.H.

BOUNCING BACK

Joan Rivers

**I've Survived Everything . . .
and I Mean Everything . . .
and You Can Too!**

B
Rive

Thorndike Press • Thorndike, Maine

Library of Congress Cataloging in Publication Data

Rivers, Joan.
   Bouncing back : I've survived everything — and I mean
everything — and you can too! / Joan Rivers.
    p. cm.
   ISBN 0-7862-0932-1 (lg. print : hc)
  1. Rivers, Joan. 2. Comedians — United States — Biography.
3. Self-help techniques. 4. Large type books. I. Title.
[PN2287.R55A3 1997a]
792.7′028′092—dc21
   [B]
                               97-5829

Acknowledgments

I warmly thank Ralph Schoenstein
for his literary help.

PRELUDE

HELLO DARKNESS,
MY OLD FRIEND

One morning three years ago, in the middle of a golf course, I asked God to strike me dead.

"Take me now," I whispered, "with a little lightning. The sun is out, but *You* don't need rain. It'll look like an act of God."

And I saw the headline: JOAN RIVERS GOES GOLFING.

At that dark moment, I thought I had excellent reasons for wanting to move to a higher realm. *Sally Marr . . . and Her Escorts*, the Tony-nominated play to which I'd given my heart for seven years, had just closed without warning after only five months. Because the whole world had seemed to like the play, I had expected it to run forever and had given up my day job, an Emmy-winning TV show.

Suddenly, for the first time in thirty years, I found myself out of show business, facing days whose highlights would be lunch. Suddenly there were no offers, no job opportunities. After thirty years of incessant work and splendid success, I was what actors like to call "at liberty." Paraphrasing Patrick Henry, I thought: Don't give me this liberty, give me death.

In late-night TV I had the future of a mosquito. David Letterman and Jay Leno continued to enforce their ten-year refusal to book me. And things were just as rosy for a new *Joan Rivers Show*. CBS had commissioned a pilot; CBS had approved the pilot; and then CBS had said, "Sorry, Joan, demographically you're too old." Chronologically, too, and I was getting older by the minute in a business that prefers you to go in the other direction.

At about the same time, Joan Rivers Products, the jewelry company that I had started and operated with great success, was forced into a bankruptcy mess, created by its parent company, Regal Communications. Regal's creditors told me that if I didn't raise the thirty-seven million dollars the company owed them, I would have to design and sell my jewelry exclusively for them until the year 2023 to pay off this debt.

There wasn't a day that the ringing of the phone didn't bring me bad news. And then the phone stopped ringing.

Yes, I thought that day on the golf course, my handicap was now life, and a kindly bolt of lightning would release me from the game. Enough was enough. How long can you keep fighting back? How often can you start again?

But with the speed of lightning, I suddenly knew that I *could* do it again: My alternate

10

career had been pulling myself up from rock bottom. I had survived being fat and poor and unwanted. I had survived being called a bitch, a no-talent, and a has-been. I had survived being told that I was unfunny, that I was too funny, that I was too young, and that I was too old. I had even survived tumbling from the top of the world into a unique hell when first the Fox network canceled my late-night talk show and then my husband Edgar committed suicide.

And when still more blows befell me, I began to envy the good luck of Job. After Edgar's death, fate tossed me not only a heartbreaking estrangement from my daughter, Melissa, but also a move to the brink of financial ruin.

I had gotten through all those ordeals. I had repaired my bond with Melissa, rebuilt my career, and created a new life for myself in New York; and so, on the day when I was hitting both a golf ball and rock bottom, I knew that I could recharge my life one more time if I used the strategies I had found seven years before.

"Excuse the call," I said to God. "I'll be staying in touch."

And I went on. In doing so, I regained full ownership of my jewelry company, which is now global; I signed a long-term contract to do specials for E! Entertainment Network; I wrote another play; and I now have concert bookings all over the world. My life in the last three years has confirmed my belief that you can get through anything. Moreover, I've been able to figure out how I survived (twice) and how *you* can too.

With this knowledge I began giving self-help seminars all over the country. In the last three years I've told thousands of people how I rebounded from an installment plan of tragedy and not only reinvented my life but made the invention worth patenting. And now I want to share the patent with you.

We all *do* learn from one another. One Ohio woman told me that her mother had just died after a long illness and, in addition, she was going through a bitter divorce.

"I was at my wit's end," she told someone who, in 1994, had felt that *her* life should be called the Wit's End. "But then I heard you speak and I realized that, just like you, I could pick myself up and start over again."

After one of my talks in Florida, a man said to me, "I've been depressed for many years. Nothing ever seems to go right for me. But tonight, for the first time, I really believe that I can turn my life around and find happiness again."

When rejecting a script, Hollywood producers have a particularly idiotic phrase: "It's in turnaround." Does this mean that the script has been put on a carousel or in a blender? However, a *life* in turnaround has joyous meaning, and I can tell you how to do it, no matter what kind of loss you've had — not because I'm so smart but because I've been there and I took notes: the Cliff Notes that'll keep you from going over one.

Perhaps your husband has just left you for another woman, one who doesn't yet know that he snores like an outboard motor. Well, I can help you start a new life, either happily single or with a man who will want to hang around. Or perhaps your home was just destroyed by a fire. I'll show you how to accept that loss as fast as your insurance company does, and how to decide on the next steps that will lead to happiness.

Whatever kind of loss has laid you low, however despondent you may feel, your pain is a very old story for the human race. Loss has been the way of the world since Adam and Eve had to leave their Garden apartment. Half of all marriages end in divorce — and then there are the really unhappy ones. Eighty percent of women will be widowed in their lifetimes. Last year one in five new businesses failed, and one in twenty Americans lost his or her job. No wonder

13

that Prozac is our favorite snack.

There are many self-help books by Ph.D.'s, but I hold a different degree: an I.B.T.I.A. — I've Been Through It All. This degree comes not on parchment but gauze, and it entitles me to tell you that there is a way to get through *any* misfortune. In these pages you'll read my no-holds-barred account of the hell I intermittently went through and how I kept surviving; and you'll meet other people who insisted on surviving too.

The fact that you've picked up this book instead of *The Wit and Wisdom of Snoop Doggy Dogg* means that you have the will to bounce back. By the time you've turned the last page, you'll have the way.

1

WHO DEALT THIS MESS?

"Mommy, Daddy killed himself."

I sat in stunned silence as Melissa broke the news to me: My husband — dead? Had committed suicide?

Suicide? Edgar? Surely it had to be some kind of mistake. Edgar and I had spoken many times about suicide, and he had always believed it to be a permanent solution to temporary problems. Could this man who had once loved life and adored his daughter have taken that life and left Melissa fatherless?

Like many people who hear bad news unexpectedly, I was in a state of disbelief. Maybe they meant another Edgar Rosenberg. Maybe this was someone's idea of a very sick joke.

How was it possible that Edgar had sunk so deep into depression that he saw no way out other than taking his own life? I wondered. How had we tumbled so very far, so very fast?

The year 1986 had begun on a high note, with the launching of *The Late Show Starring Joan Rivers* on the new Fox-TV network. Edgar and I were both ecstatic. The show was our reward for twenty-five years of hard work. It was the payoff for my long years in

17

tiny comedy clubs; the endless one-nighters, alone in hotel rooms away from my family for weeks at a time; and then my slow, steady climb to stardom. It was the return on all the planning and wisdom and love Edgar had poured into my career.

My husband and I had always worked wonderfully together, I on stage and Edgar behind the scenes. And so, when Fox offered me my own late-night talk show, he and I assumed that our partnership would continue to be as fine as ever. However, Edgar and Barry Diller, the chairman and CEO of Fox, disliked and distrusted each other from the start. When the show didn't quickly live up to the network's expectations, Diller and his colleagues graciously blamed Edgar.

A proud man's pride had been shattered, in spite of my efforts to protect both Edgar and the show. In June, Fox canceled *The Late Show With Joan Rivers* and issued press releases that were a family two-cushion shot: They vilified Edgar and humiliated me.

In the months that followed, Edgar suffered greatly and changed from a secure man into a self-doubting, bitter, and depressed one. The doctors didn't realize it at the time, but the medication he had been taking since his heart attack in 1984 was creating a chemical imbalance that led to deep depression. That condition, combined with the stress and humiliation he had faced at Fox, broke Edgar's spirit. He was angry all the time and frequently turned his anger on me. His black moods lasted longer and longer, until they were no longer moods but an endless despondency.

It was so painful for me to see Edgar in such misery — painful and frightening. What had happened to the man I had known and loved for so many years? What was going to happen to him if he didn't get help immediately? All that summer I tried desperately to convince him to get psychiatric care, something beyond his occasional talks with a psychologist, but he ignored my pleas. On August 10 I returned home from a trip to New York and called Edgar to tell him I had landed safely in Los Angeles. During that phone call I again mentioned psychiatric care. And again he refused.

Finally I had to accept the fact that Edgar was a drowning man, and that he was taking me down with him, to the bottom of a sea of despair where I could be no good to him, to myself, or to our daughter. I was so weary of fighting him, so tired of trying to help someone who refused my outstretched hand and my support, that I simply did not know how I could continue.

"Edgar," I heard myself say, "if you won't agree to get psychiatric help, I'm not coming home to you."

And I didn't. I went straight to the Century Plaza hotel, where, exhausted and tearful, I fell asleep in my clothes.

The next day Edgar flew to Philadelphia to see his best friend and business adviser, Tom Pileggi. Phoning from there, Edgar told me that he had done a lot of thinking; and he promised that, when he returned to Beverly Hills, he would at last get treatment for his clinical depression. He was lying, of course.

Later that night he spoke to Melissa on the phone, said he was feeling optimistic for the first time in a long time, and was eager to get home. She was the last person to speak to him. And he was lying to her, too: He had already made plans to take his life.

After Edgar's suicide Melissa and I told ourselves, with agonizing guilt, that we shouldn't have believed him when he'd said he was okay. I kept saying that we should have had someone guard him day and night until he came home and admitted himself to a hospital; and Melissa felt guilty that she had not said something on the phone to stop him.

However, I have learned, through my work

with other suicide survivors, that if someone really wants to kill him- or herself, that person will do it — after convincing everyone he or she is okay.

And Edgar *had* convinced us. He had made all of us believe that he was feeling well and optimistic again. Melissa and I had allowed ourselves to be optimistic, too. She had spent time with her friends and had started getting ready for her sophomore year at the University of Pennsylvania; and I had gone into the hospital for some minor cosmetic surgery, thinking that feeling good about my appearance would help me recover from some of the battering my ego had taken since *The Late Show* was canceled. I imagined that when I got home from the hospital and Edgar returned from Philadelphia, we would once again be happy, mutually supportive, and ready to face life's challenges.

But the news Melissa brought me that morning shattered all those hopes. Edgar had overdosed on Valium and Librium, and had washed the pills down with a miniature bottle of Scotch from his hotel room's minibar. I wanted to believe that his overdose was accidental, but Melissa told me her father had left three audio cassettes — one for her, one for me, and one for Tom Pileggi. The police had transcribed the tapes

21

and there was no doubt: Edgar's death had been a suicide.

Even with that evidence, I still needed time to believe what I was hearing. And these days, as I travel around the country giving my lectures, I learn over and over again that disbelief is an almost universal initial reaction to bad news:

"When I heard the storm warnings before Hurricane Andrew hit," says a woman named Karen, who told her stories at one of my survival lectures, "I took the kids to my sister's place, away from the eye of the storm. I watched the news coverage on TV in Terri's living room and saw the houses on my street wash away. And still I couldn't believe it. I thought somehow my own home would be spared, or that I was just in the middle of a horrible dream."

It was only after the storm, when Karen went back to her old neighborhood and saw for herself that her home was gone, that the reality began to sink in.

"My home had been destroyed. There was simply nothing salvageable left. And yet I had to go back three times before I really believed it."

Her behavior was not unusual. When something dreadful happens, people often go for second, third, and even fourth opinions before accepting the blow.

"When our doctor told us my wife had breast cancer," says a man named Mike, "we called my brother-in-law, who's a doctor, to have him check the mammogram. Then Marla went for three more mammograms, hoping they would discover that the first diagnosis had been a mistake."

And even when they believe the news, many people expect a reversal of the fact:

"My husband told me he was having an affair," says a woman named Betty, "and I believed it. But for months I kept thinking that Steve would get tired of his fling, that it was just a midlife crisis and that he would come back to our marriage."

"When I was fired from my job with no notice," says a man named Len, "I packed up my desk and took my belongings home. But for the next three weeks, I expected the phone to ring and my boss to tell me that the company couldn't get along without me, that they wanted me back."

"Denial is a common defense mechanism that works by preventing a person from recognizing or experiencing information that is threatening to their self-preservation," says Susan Bodnar, Ph.D., a psychotherapist. "Denial also serves to protect you from anxiety."

But while denying bad news may *seem* to make life easier by shielding us from pain, it also prevents us from dealing with the pain. And if you can't deal with it, you can't push forward.

"I wouldn't accept that my mother was dying," says a woman named Mindy. "If I *had* faced it, I would have spent more special days with her. It was only when she came back from her last surgery that I realized she was really dying. By then she didn't have much time left."

Today Mindy is more realistic about bad news. Like many of us, she has learned painfully that accepting reality is the only way to deal with it. Then you can force yourself to make decisions, meet new challenges, and grieve for losses.

If you're having trouble accepting the full impact of what you're facing, make a written account of what has happened to you. Make a list. In fact, keep a pad with you as you read this book to help you *do* the exercises I suggest; don't just think about them: Take out some paper or a notebook and in a few short sentences, write down the basic headlines of your challenge or your loss.

If I had known to do this after Edgar's suicide, my statement would have looked like this:

My husband of twenty-two years killed himself. My career is over. I am a widow, and my daughter, the most important person on earth to me, is now fatherless. Despite the fact that we live in a big house and have nice things, we are, because of bad investments, nearly broke.

Shorter than *War and Peace* and not as funny.

Notice that I say Edgar "killed himself," not "passed away" or "left us." Our shiftless doorman "left us"; Edgar killed himself. I say "unemployed," not "between positions." "Between positions" is a couple taking a pause during sex. All those euphemisms are fine for someone else's loss; but in accepting your own, use the simplest and bluntest words. Dead. Raped. Cancer. Betrayed. The words may stick in your throat, but using them will help you to confront the truth of your situation and start to move you forward.

Mark Twain said, "Always tell the truth. It will please some people and astonish the rest." Accepting the full reality of your blow will help you to begin the important work of grieving, force you to spring into action to handle a crisis. But for your recovery to be complete, you need to understand not only the objective facts — death, illness,

25

destruction of property — but also what your situation means to you and how it will affect your life.

So go back to your notebook and write down all the ways your loss is affecting you, not only the big but also the little ways it hurts.

If your parents have both died, you may think: Orphan. But what does that really mean? Does it mean no more heart-to-heart talks with your mother? Does it mean you'll have to spend every Thanksgiving at your in-laws' from now on? To mourn your loss properly, you have to understand what it means to you.

It certainly doesn't mean that you'll never smile again, although at first you might not agree with Oscar Wilde: "To lose one parent . . . may be regarded as a misfortune. To lose both looks like carelessness." When Edgar died, a lot of people looked at me with pity and thought: Widow. And, to tell the truth, that's the way I thought of myself at first: part of Hallmark's gloomiest section. It was only in the weeks and months after Edgar's death that I realized that every widow's experiences are as unique as the marriage she had.

When I really thought about what I had lost with Edgar's death, I looked back on twenty-two years of marriage. Ours was the kind you rarely see in Hollywood: genuine, deep, and abiding. We loved each other and our daughter, we loved the life we had built for ourselves, and the way we had seamlessly blended career and family. Like any couple, we had our fights and rough times. But we were as good a team as two people who live and work together can be.

I was going to miss that partnership, that sense of knowing someone so well that I could finish his sentences.

And I was going to miss lots of little things about Edgar, things I never thought about until they were gone forever. For one thing, he was a very educated, interesting man. And I, who always worried whether people would think I was smart enough, had come to rely on Edgar to keep me from being consumed by insecurity. No matter where we went, I never had to worry about what topic was coming up. Whatever people were talking about, Edgar had an intelligent comment and would always say, "Joan and I think . . ." so that I would feel both smart and secure. People find it hard to believe, but I am terribly shy. Edgar's death meant I would have to work through my shyness and go out alone and talk to people one-on-one.

I also missed Edgar on a very practical level. He wasn't only my best friend, lover, and partner but he was the man who knew how to balance the checkbook, program the VCR, and park the car; I could do none of those things. Truly accepting my loss meant that I was going to have to take Accounting for Nitwits at the same time I was learning to live without my best friend. While learning how to conquer loneliness, I would also have to learn how to stop being the kind of woman who would invest in the Venus de Milo Massage Center.

Some of the details of your loss may seem insignificant or even petty. Of course there is no way to compare the frustration of having to set the clock on the VCR with the loss of your life partner. But accepting all the sad *and* "silly" ways your loss affects you is one key to moving beyond that loss.

Having learned that lesson with Edgar's death, I realized, when I was hit with devastating professional losses two years ago, that I needed to know exactly what had happened, why it had, and what it had meant. In spite of what had sent me reeling, I needed to feel that I could again somehow become the master of my professional life.

After the Fox cancellation and Edgar's death, I had worked my way back into show business, starting with small TV appearances, until I was finally starring in a Broadway play, *Sally Marr . . . and Her Escorts.* With Edgar's initial help, I'd been working on this play for seven years; and when it finally clicked, the sound wasn't a click but a bang. Moments after the first reading, we got our production money. I hired a brilliant young director named Lonny Price and first-rate supporting players. When the curtain went up for the opening at the Helen Hayes Theater, on May 5, 1994, it was theatrical magic. The audience laughed and cried where I wanted them to, and the reviews sounded as though I'd written them myself. When I was nominated for a Tony, I thought: This is finally it. My life is wonderful for the first time since Edgar's death.

With that giddy optimism, I made plans to take the show to Los Angeles, London, and Australia. *Sally Marr* was going to run longer than World War II.

There was, however, one problem: Though the show's raves were going through the roof, so were its expenses, and we were barely breaking even. We had started out with one piano; by the time we opened, we were headed for the Philharmonic. Moreover, we had four rear projectionists. Do you know how much that costs? Neither did I.

Without Edgar I was a financial idiot; I thought a debenture straightened your teeth. A supporting cast that had begun as a few shadow people dressed in black was now changing costumes like ladies at Saks. Soon, we had three dressers and two hairdressers — fine for *Aïda* but financial madness for the small theater we were in. And one black day I learned that there was no way to keep the show open. I felt a nightmarish unreality at seeing it closed with two days' notice.

I was heartbroken. In show business I had always operated on the notion that you must have a dozen balloons in the air at all times because eleven of them will probably burst. This time, though, I'd been waltzing along with just one balloon. And suddenly the air went out of me, too; I was so devastated that I couldn't speak to Lonny, our director, for a year because I knew that the sound of his voice would bring back everything I'd poured into the play: hard work, pride, and a belief I could rise from the ashes like a phoenix. Instead of being a phoenix, I'd become a dead duck.

"I just can't talk to you," I said in a message on Lonny's answering machine. "It hurts too much."

In the days that followed, I got out my pad and pencil and spelled out my loss, which is what *you* have to do. Knowing why *Sally Marr* meant so much to me was the first step in grieving for its demise.

The play had been the center of my life. For seven years it had absorbed me professionally and emotionally. Because I'd thought it would run forever, I had walked away from my daytime talk show, canceled concert tours and stand-up bookings in Las Vegas, and turned down the chance to star in a situation comedy. And now, for the first time since 1968, I had no place to go every day. There is no prospect bleaker. A person must have a reason to get up in the morning, and now I had none; I was unemployed.

In losing my job, I'd also lost my audience. Performers become performers because we crave an audience's love. And doing a play was even more intoxicating than doing stand-up comedy: You make the audience believe that you *are* the character. Becoming Sally Marr had been particularly challenging for me because the audience had always known me as Joan. When Sally was onstage, I'd felt the audience was responding to her and *not* to Joan. The explosive applause at the end of each show had confirmed my belief.

And the show was more than heady stuff for me: It was also a valentine to the mother of my professional godfather, if you can follow that fractured genealogy. Sally Marr was the mother of Lenny Bruce; and if it hadn't been for him, I might be an Avon lady today.

In the 1960s, when I started telling my jokes in Greenwich Village coffee shops, the insiders all were telling me, "You can't say that, Joan. You're a woman."

I was not unaware of my gender. In a routine about how I got into show business, I used to say: "How do I get booked? My talent? No, I just go into the agent's office and say, 'Hi, I'm Joan Rivers and I put out.' "

In the late sixties no woman said such things in public. No woman said that when she had her baby, she screamed for twenty-three hours straight — and that was just during the conception.

And certainly no white woman came on-stage after a black male singer and said at the end of his applause: "I'm so glad you like my husband's act."

Critics felt that such jokes entitled me to another line of work, perhaps in a delicatessen.

Meanwhile, Lenny Bruce had been doing outrageous, no-holds-barred comedy and getting praise for it. So I went to watch his show and learn. And one night Lenny came to see *me* perform, and he sent me a note backstage that said with simple eloquence: "Joan, you're right, they're wrong."

I still have that note. Lenny believed in me when few others did, and his encouragement gave me the confidence to follow my own instincts and tell the jokes that I wanted to tell. And so the play I wrote about Lenny's mother was all tied up with my feelings for Lenny himself, and with my rise from the small stages of tiny clubs to the big Vegas shows and Carson.

Later, when Lenny was vilified and couldn't work, I met Sally Marr for the first time and liked her from the first moment. Sally was a woman who had done everything on her own, at a time when Betty Friedan was still asking her husband what he wanted for dinner.

"Let's do a play about Sally," I told Edgar, and we began to interview her. When I listened to those tapes as I began to work on the show after Edgar's death, I could hear his voice, happy and excited. In that way *Sally Marr* linked me to the Edgar I had loved and worked with for so many years before his depression set in. And so, when the play closed, I had to face the fact that I would never again have a project that had been mine and Edgar's together. This was truly the end of our twenty-two-year partnership in life, love, and business, and I grieved profoundly for that loss.

It wasn't easy, but having a concrete list of what I was grieving for made the whole process of loss and recovery easier. The same list-making method helped me get through the loss of my jewelry business, which happened at the same time that *Sally Marr* closed.

In 1991 a new home-shopping cable channel called QVC had approached me about selling face cream. "The way I look," I'd replied, "they'll buy it only if it's a vanishing cream."

We decided that jewelry would be better for me, so I started designing and selling it on the air. Simple pieces: pearl-and-gold button earrings; a single strand of faux pearls; a gold-toned watch; the kind of basic pieces you'd need if you were stranded somewhere and had nothing — the Gilligan's Island Collection. Actually we called it the Joan Rivers Classics Collection, and it came to me when I was wondering if someone might have to take up a collection for *me.*

However, my designs turned out to be enormously popular, and my company quickly grew. My signature piece was the gold-toned-and-crystal bumblebee you see me wearing on the jacket of this book. Aeronautical engineers have studied bumblebees for years and said that their structure and wing size should make them unable to fly. Well, the bumblebee, defying all the laws of aeronautics, *does* fly. It achieves the impossible, and so it has been my mascot for many years.

In 1993 QVC was taken over by Barry Diller, who had fired me at Fox in 1987.

"Take the business public," said Tom Pileggi, my trusted adviser. "Get your money now, and you won't have to worry if Barry decides to fire you again."

Tom had met a man called Arthur Toll, who held the controlling interest in a publicly owned company called Regal Communications. The company was engaged in marketing a variety of products on television through infomercials. It also had developed and produced a series of telephone programs for the consumer market. When Toll offered me sixteen million dollars in Regal stock for my company, it seemed like a perfect fit and a great opportunity.

Tom and my other advisers told me to accept the offer at once. Sixteen million dollars? They didn't have to tell me twice. With that kind of money, Melissa and I would be secure for the rest of our lives. Like many people who've been rocked by a major financial loss, I'd become deeply concerned about security; and so I made the deal, even though the terms of the merger of my company into Regal required me to sign away control of the company and give up any rights I had to market my jewelry and other products, except through Regal, till the year 2023. But I wasn't worried; my company was strong.

And then one day my broker called and told me that Regal Communications stock was slipping fast. A nineteen-million-dollar debt had surfaced, and Regal had issued thirty-seven million dollars' worth of bonds, using my company as collateral.

Almost immediately, creditors were after my autograph — on checks. Because mine was the only healthy company Regal owned, they felt that I was liable for the thirty-seven million dollars it owed to other investors. The bondholders told me that they owned the rights to my name and all my income from jewelry and product sales into the coming century. Any profit from the jewelry business or other products would be theirs, as would any earnings from television, movies, commercials, infomercials, or book deals. And if I couldn't raise the thirty-seven million dollars, I wouldn't be allowed to design my jewelry or market other products with my name, except as a slave to Regal.

How did a nice Jewish girl end up with the national debt of Nicaragua?

I cried for days. Work had always been my way of proving to myself and the world that I had something to contribute. Having my father's strong work ethic, I was overwhelmed by guilt at being unemployed; and being in debt left me terrified.

As I wrote down my feelings about the bankruptcy, I admitted that I'd been stupid for having let myself be drawn into a bad deal; and I was insanely angry at the people who had led me into the mess. Like most women of my generation, I had grown up expecting a man to take care of me and make all the right financial decisions, as Edgar had always done. But now I knew that I could rely only on myself. It was time to learn things I had never paid attention to, and to take responsibility for my own life. The magnitude of that responsibility had me reeling.

Whatever loss has hit you, look hard at it to figure out what you're really losing. That's the only way to get over it.

"About a year after I got married," says a woman named Meghan, a young lawyer in Chicago, "my husband told me he was leaving for a while. That afternoon I went to the cash machine and I saw that our entire account had been cleared out. I called the bank and discovered that Bob had also taken all the money out of our savings and investments and had run our credit card bills up to the max, leaving me liable because my name was on the accounts too. Walking home with an empty wallet, I realized that Bob had left for good. All I did for three days was sit on my couch and cry.

"But finally," says Meghan, "I had to admit that the marriage had never felt like a real one to me, and I wasn't that sorry to have it over. Having him gone was actually a huge relief to me. So then why was I sitting on my couch sobbing? I was forced to take a good hard look at what had been going on in our marriage. And then I filed for divorce.

"There I was," says Meghan, "twenty-nine years old and all of a sudden I had this label — divorced — a scandal in my Catholic family.

"I was also upset about the way the divorce would make me the object of office gossip at my law firm. Well, once I admitted to myself that *those* were my big concerns, and not any feelings about Bob himself, I could gather the strength to tell my friends that Bob and I had split, and then go into work with my head held high. By taking a good hard look at what was bothering me about the divorce, I could deal with each emotion individually and cope with each loss on its own. Freeing myself in that way allowed me to stop mourning and move into action by hiring the best feminist lawyer I could find and getting Bob to pay me my share of the money he'd stolen."

As Meghan discovered, your strongest feelings about your loss may have to do not with the "headlines" of that loss, but with the subtext. Her feelings about divorce involved more than missing her husband.

No matter what you've lost, figure out its real meaning and all its ramifications.

"The news 'you'll never walk again' is so overwhelming," says a man named Kevin, who was in a diving accident when he was seventeen. "As the news sunk in, I realized that being a paraplegic was a lot more than not walking. It meant no more touch football, which I played so often with my friends; now I'd be cut off from them. It meant that I'd have to pick a college open to wheelchairs. It meant knowing the girls who'd been dying to go out with me when I was captain of the swim team wouldn't be caught dead with me now. I had to change my whole life."

Even material losses can have complex emotional repercussions: "When I saw the rubble after the hurricane," says Karen, "I just sat there crying, 'My house, my house, my house.' By the next day, I realized that my tears were about more than just not having a roof over my head. I had lost control of my life. My sense of security was gone. I felt horribly alone."

But Karen admits there were some hidden blessings to the hurricane: "Three years earlier, my husband had dumped me for another woman from the neighborhood. Ever since, I'd always felt that people were gossiping about me. My kids were subject to the gossip too. But I felt that we had to hold our heads up. I wanted to teach the kids that you don't run away from your problems.

"And so, after the hurricane, I was happy to have a good excuse to move across town, where no one knew us."

Be honest with yourself about any way in which your loss may actually bring some kind of relief. That kind of honesty may sound cold-blooded, but it's also part of the healing process.

For example, Edgar's death freed me from having to stay in California after Fox canceled my TV show. Edgar was a proud man. I knew that if he had lived, we would have stayed prisoners in Beverly Hills (not the worst place, of course, to do time), refusing to admit defeat, move away, and start over. As bereft as his death left me, it also left me able to say: Where do I go now? What do I do? Who do I want to be? At first I felt guilt at enjoying those thoughts, but there was no way to get around it: There *were* some little ways in which Edgar's death opened options for me that I wouldn't have had if he'd been alive.

Can you be that brutally, painfully honest about your situation? A lot of people can't. I've seen so many widows turn their late husbands into a combination of Einstein and Jesus Christ. Along with the husband they bury the memory of the time he cheated, or the annoying way his teeth clicked when he ate, or how he never helped with the house-work. But remembering loved ones as we wish they had been instead of how they really were makes it impossible to complete our emotional relationship with them.

That's why I was pleased recently to see a young man get up at his father's funeral and say: "As you all know, my dad could be a real pain in the neck, but he was a lovable pain in the neck and we're all going to miss him." He went on to talk about his father's stubbornness, but then about how wonderful he was with kids and all the unheralded acts of charity he had performed during his life. That was one of the most moving eulogies I've ever heard — and one of the healthiest.

Does calling your dad a pain in the neck mean you didn't adore him? Of course not. Does acknowledging your husband's faults mean you didn't love him? Absolutely not. And the purpose of this exercise is not to convince yourself that your loss is the best thing that ever happened to you. However, the more realistic you are about your loss, the better you'll be able to cope and the more healing will be your time of mourning.

You don't want to be like Queen Victoria, who mourned the death of her husband for the last forty years of her long life. What a difference it might have made if someone had simply gone to her and said, "Your Royal Highness, get a life."

2

YOUR RIGHT TO SING
THE BLUES

After a bad shock or loss, give yourself time and permission to grieve in *whatever* way is natural for you. Don't suppress or deny your feelings; in fact, take some time to wallow in them, for you'll be full of complex and confusing emotions that you have to sort out. But keep your wallowing *short*.

Don't worry if you're grieving properly; propriety has nothing to do with grief. The actress Mariette Hartley, whose father killed himself when she was a teenager, often said to Melissa and me, "Grief is not graceful. I cried all the time. I wasn't exactly Jackie Onassis."

From the moment that Melissa and I returned from Edgar's funeral, the house was filled with both friends and strangers, all trying to buffer us from our pain. Unfortunately, I had to be buffered from the pain of some of *them*. One friend of Edgar's went to my husband's closet, put on one of his hats, and wandered through the house saying, "Anyone mind if I take this?" He was a man who couldn't tell the difference between a wake and a garage sale.

Only to a chemist is blood always thicker than water. At times of grief, good friends can be better than bad relations. Let in only people who will boost you, not sap you.

And also find time to be alone to cope with your feelings. For me that time would come late at night, after the last visitors had left. Alone in my bedroom, I thought about Edgar and all the dreams we had shared. I cried for Melissa, for everything she had lost much too soon and too horribly. Being alone with those thoughts was very painful, but it was as important to my mourning as the time I spent with friends.

In confronting a loss, you too must carve out private time for yourself, even if your friends or obligations make it hard for you to take such private retreats.

Just remember: Surviving is the best revenge, no matter what the disaster has been. As a character in one of Stephen Sondheim's shows triumphantly sings, "I'm still here."

At one of my lectures, a woman wanted to know what she should do now that her husband had left her and her seven-year-old child for another woman after cleaning out their bank account.

"Son of a bitch!" I cried, triggering applause. "Okay, it's done, now move on. *Move on.* And don't take the piece of slime back — unless you get everything in your name."

There was more laughter and applause.

"Life is a movie," I tell them, "and you're the star. Give it a happy ending."

While the extent and duration of your emotions will vary with your particular loss, the feelings and the mourning process are always similar. You are likely to feel angry, guilty, confused, and overwhelmed. Allow yourself these feelings, don't fight them, and you'll heal faster.

Taking time is important, no matter who or what you have lost, as I learned from the parallels of my two different ordeals of loss and recovery. Edgar's suicide, of course, is the worst thing I've ever faced. However, I was surprised to learn that the combination of the demise of *Sally Marr* and the loss of my jewelry business left me with similar feelings of mourning. Losing both was a kind of little death for me.

Edgar, *Sally Marr*, Arthur Toll . . . my life had become a soap opera, one I was trying to have canceled and replaced by *As Joan Turns*.

Mariette Hartley was right about grieving not being graceful, but some people have trouble doing it at all. I do a comedy bit about the different ways that WASPs and Italians handle death. Of course, it's an exaggeration to the point of absurdity, and it gets a laugh; but in some cultures, the mes-

47

sages *are* "keep a stiff upper lip" and "big boys don't cry."

"From the time I was three years old," says Mike, "my father told me to 'take things like a man.' So when I found out my wife, Marla, had breast cancer, I didn't let myself cry. The thought of breaking down was almost as frightening to me as everything else that was going on. What if I started crying and couldn't stop? Marla would think I was weak. But I realize now that holding in those feelings didn't help me, but just made it harder for me to deal with my own pain and harder for me to be there for my wife."

Expressing grief is not only emotionally healthy, say doctors, but better for your body too. So go ahead and indulge yourself in a good, *brief* wallow. Hide under the covers for forty-eight hours. Do nothing but savor self-pity. Make lists of everyone who ever hurt you, of every rotten thing that's ever happened to you. Bestsellers are born that way.

When I make *my* self-pity list, I start with not being picked to be a healthy tooth in my first-grade Dental Day pageant; I was an abscess. And I was so fat that, later, on the back of my gym suit it said PASS and DON'T PASS. It was no surprise that I couldn't get a date for my senior prom. My mother said, "Don't worry, your cousin will take you."

But he wouldn't and I had to go alone.

I write down every slight, every hurt, and of course the real injustices, too, to help purge myself of the pain. After a while, it all seems comical. I can't be Tolstoy about what happened to me when I did my act at a seedy Boston bar for $125 a week in 1964 under the name Pepper January.

After the first show, the manager came over to me and said, "Hey, Pep — you don't have any. You're fired."

And then, as I was packing up to go home from my seedy hotel room, my agent called and said, "I'm dumping you, Babe, but I'm keeping the name. Women comics I can always find, but not a name like Pepper January."

How's that for pouring salt in Pepper's wound?

And how about you? Still feeling bad that you were picked last for kickball in the second grade? Write it down. Don't cross it out or say, "How can I complain about kickball when there are children starving in Africa?" This isn't a bravery contest, it's a festival of self-pity. You own the list and no one else will ever see it, so feel sorry for yourself for everything, including your last six parking tickets.

And, of course, be sure to write down

what sent you to bed in the first place. Your sister-in-law's tragic death. Your marital breakup. Your wife's breast cancer. The time you spend wallowing will actually shorten your recovery time. You'll certainly want to get up pretty soon and change those sheets.

3

GOOD MOURNING

From the moment I heard about Edgar's suicide, many different emotions kept me from thinking clearly. First, I was overcome by despair: Edgar had always been my best friend, and losing my best friend was unthinkable. Could he really be gone?

I was also overwhelmed by guilt: What if I had gone home the night of August 10 instead of going to a hotel? What if I had tried one more time to persuade Edgar to get help? Now I would never have the chance.

And then came the anger: How could Edgar leave me and Melissa after everything we'd been through? How could he do it in Philadelphia, knowing that when Melissa returned to the University of Pennsylvania in September, she would have to pass the scene of his suicide on every trip downtown? And he had done it when I was out of the house! Hadn't he known that Melissa would be the one to hear the news? The thought that he hadn't at least shielded our daughter from that horror enraged me.

At first I tried to hold that anger in. But, as Geoffrey Gorer writes in *Death, Grief and Mourning*, "Although our culture gives no symbolic expression to anger, a considerable number of others have done so. Rituals included destruction of the dead person's possessions."

Gorer must have been peeking through my library window. When my anger finally became unbearable, I kicked Edgar's desk so hard that I nearly broke a toe. At first I felt guilty about being angry, but I've since learned that it's all right and even healthy to feel anger at someone who has died, whether from suicide, sickness, or old age.

And so I cursed and threw things. I opened Edgar's medicine chest, grabbed his pills, and created a flying pharmacy. As much as I missed Edgar and grieved for him, I was furious at him for willfully leaving me — and, much worse, his daughter.

And Melissa was very angry too. However, if she and I had known then about the rage that suicide leaves in its wake, we would have felt less guilty about our anger at Edgar — and been less likely to turn it on each other.

So learn from our mistake and be honest with yourself about your anger.

"For a few weeks after Steve left, I couldn't stand to be around anybody else," says Betty, whose husband came home one night after twenty-eight years of marriage and told her he was leaving with his twenty-four-year-old girlfriend. "Suddenly I found myself snapping at people who were trying to support me. It took me a while to realize that I wasn't mad at them, but at Steven. And maybe at myself, too, for putting up with his philandering for so many years. Finally I went around the house and smashed all the pictures of the two of us together. It was incredibly cathartic and it helped me focus my anger where it belonged, instead of taking it out on well-meaning friends."

If you don't feel in a smashing mood, pour out all your anger and bitterness onto a piece of paper. Write a letter to the person or persons who have wronged you. And then put the letters aside in a safe place: Do *not* mail them. Writing unsent letters of rage is a harmless way to acknowledge your anger. Trust me: A year or so later, you'll gladly tear them up.

President Harry S. Truman used to write such letters, and then his wife, Bess, would read them, say, "Okay, Harry, you've gotten that out of your system," and tear them up. She missed only one: the threatening letter that Truman wrote to the music critic of the *Washington Post* who had panned Margaret Truman's singing. The president had quickly mailed that one himself, and the world soon learned of a famous father's love for his daughter.

Writing your poison-pen letters to the people you're angry at, no matter how silly it makes you feel at first, is a great safety valve. Start writing as fast as you can; speed will keep your inner censor from reminding you to be polite. Write down all the anger, all the unsettled scores, and then let go of the anger and move on, or else the person who wronged you will have dealt you a deeper defeat.

An angry letter *can* have style. Benjamin Franklin once told a man off and finished the letter by saying:

You, sir, are my enemy and I am

Yours,
B. Franklin

But, unlike Franklin, you don't have to start a revolution. Just stand up for yourself with honesty and guts. And you'll need some of those guts to go against the crowd — a decision that puts you out of step in America today, where being a victim is the height of fashion. You won't be one of the millions who know whom to blame for their misfortune: their mothers, their teachers, their bosses, their United Parcel men. Our favorite sound is whining; our new national anthem should be "Don't Blame Me."

If you make yourself a professional victim, you won't survive. Your father abused you when you were seven? You're now fifty-three. Terrible as the act was, that's long enough to reminisce. Either drop it and move on, or get into therapy and move on. Have no nostalgia for misery.

After the loss of my TV show, *Sally Marr*, and my jewelry business, I was totally out of work for the second time in thirty years — and I was now *sixty years old*. When I had entered show business, as Pepper January, my father had said I would fall on my face. And he was right. He just hadn't known that it would be a very slow drop.

However, when I did hit bottom, the only thing I could think of doing had been set down by lyricist Dorothy Fields: pick myself up, dust myself off, and start all over again. Dr. Kevorkian will get no call from me, unless I think he'd look good in a brooch.

Sometimes others *are* to blame for your misfortune, but you still can't throw up your hands in defeat, a lesson I learned from an old friend, the noted actor Roddy McDowall.

In the 1940s Roddy was a child star in such films as *How Green Was My Valley* and

Lassie Come Home. On his seventeenth birthday, however, he was summoned by Louis B. Mayer, the head of MGM, who said, "Here's your contract back, son. We don't want you anymore. You're too old."

At *seventeen!*

Telling himself, I'm not finished, Roddy went to New York and began auditioning for shows, never too proud to call a producer and ask for a chance to read. And soon he got parts in such hits as *No Time for Sergeants*, *Compulsion*, and *Camelot*; and then he went on to become a fine photographer.

At last Hollywood woke up, and Roddy returned to star in more than a hundred films, including *Planet of the Apes* and *Murder on the Orient Express.*

As Roddy knew, moving on is a gift you give yourself. In show business the same people come around again and again — a kind of executive recycling — so you have to learn to put your anger behind you because last year's enemy is this year's colleague.

In 1987, as the head of Fox TV, Barry Diller had canceled my show and had become a face for Edgar and me to decorate with darts. Six years later, when I was in the jewelry business, Diller became the head of QVC, and I once again recognized the truth of the ancient Persian saying: Keep your hate list in pencil.

In 1993 I was in a hotel room in London when the telephone rang.

"Hello, Joan," said a voice. "It's Barry Diller. Sit down. I hope you're laughing: I'm your boss again."

The moment Barry said, "I hope you're laughing," I knew we were in a new relationship. It was six years later and time to move forward. I had learned that there comes a time when you have to let go of grudges. If you always want to work only with lovely people, open the *Yellow Pages* to CONVENTS.

As you struggle to let go of your anger, let go of your guilt as well, whether or not that guilt is deserved. If your loss *was* partly your fault, admit it, of course.

Joan, I had to say to myself, you never should have let the costs of *Sally Marr* get so out of hand. And before signing over your business in a stock merger, you should have checked to see if Arthur Toll was managing Regal properly. And you shouldn't have suggested that separation from Edgar. What if you had checked more often with his psychiatrist?

And then, like a defendant with a good

59

lawyer, walk away from the guilt and move on, for there is absolutely no pastime as fruitless and foolish as replaying the past. You can never know for sure how much of it *you* caused and how much was caused by the gods who have such sport with us.

So don't drive yourself crazy. Instead, think about the wonderful prayer written by the theologian Reinhold Niebuhr:

> . . . God grant me the serenity to accept the things I cannot change, the courage to change the things I can, and the wisdom to know the difference.

Once you've acknowledged your mistakes, learn from them while moving forward, the only sensible direction to go. Ralph Waldo Emerson made this point in the best way I have ever read:

> Finish every day and be done with it. You have done what you could. Some blunders and absurdities no doubt crept in; forget them as soon as you can. Tomorrow is a new day; begin it well and serenely and with too high a spirit to be encumbered with your old nonsense. This day is all that is good and fair. It is too dear, with its hopes and invita-

tions, to waste a moment on the yester-days.

After Edgar's death Melissa also was haunted by guilt. She tortured herself by wondering if there was something she could have said in their last phone conversation that might have made him decide not to take his life. And my own demons, of course, kept blaming me for not going to Philadelphia. How foolish the two of us were! Is *any* human endeavor more foolish and fruitless than replaying the past? When you see the film of President Kennedy in Dallas, do you expect a different ending?

At last both Melissa and I had to accept the awful fact that Edgar had planned to kill himself. He had other options, but he chose the one that Melissa and I simply could not prevent. There was no Clarence, Jimmy Stewart's angel, watching Philadelphia that night to show Edgar that he'd really had a wonderful life.

And so let me warn you: The game of might-have-been is one that's popular at the funny farm. Life is too random, too unfair, and too absurd to think that we can ever control more than half of it; almost everything we do involves luck. Caesar's Palace may have organized its luck, but you and I can't.

"All life is eight-to-five against," said Damon Runyon.

So what? Let me keep showing you how to beat those odds. Let me keep showing you how to bet.

4

LIKE SINATRA, DO IT *YOUR* WAY

The first rule of survival is: Make your own rules. The *hell* with what anyone thinks about the way you're acting; listen only to yourself. And while listening, remember the words of Nietzsche: "Whatever doesn't kill me makes me stronger."

Since your loss didn't kill you, it *has* made you stronger and has also given you the right to respond to it in any way you damn please. The loss may have been a universal one, but your circumstances are unique, so don't let anyone tell you how you should feel or behave. Keep fighting in your own way — with courage, with humor, and without shame. And my credentials for giving you this rule are: I'm an authority on how to keep going when things look hopeless. I've been up and down all my life; I'm the queen of the yo-yos.

Naturally, as unique individuals, Melissa and I handled our grief about Edgar in different ways. At first, unable to sleep, we both drifted through the house in silence. At last, one night, she came into the library where I was sitting and put her head in my lap, just as she'd done when she was a little girl.

Soon afterward, however, the tension between us began, for Melissa was still a teenager and resented being suddenly hurled into adult responsibilities. Resenting what the suicide had done to her, she turned her anger on me; and then, both angry and confused, she began to withdraw, while I came out of my shell and talked and joked endlessly to the well-wishers who filled the house. At a wake mourners are encouraged to feel a certain traditional merriness, but Jews mourn at what is called a shiva.

At the shiva, I still was able to laugh, but Melissa went deeper into her shell, which profoundly upset me. She was appalled by my telling jokes just hours after Edgar's funeral. Where were my tears? Her response was a refusal to be with the people. What she didn't understand was that my feelings were so overwhelming that I was able to deal with them only in the way that I had always dealt with pain: by laughing through my tears.

One night, after the week of shiva had ended, Melissa and I walked into a Los Angeles restaurant. Everyone was staring at us, waiting for us to order hemlock cocktails or stab ourselves with our salad forks. But we held our heads high; and when I opened the menu, I said, "If Daddy saw these prices, he'd kill himself all over again!"

For the first time since the suicide, Melissa laughed. Anger left her eyes, and I saw the old sparkle there. I also saw every head in the restaurant turn toward us disapprovingly.

Her husband dead a week and they're *laughing!*

These people don't want to see us heal, I thought. They just want to judge us on their own terms. They're angry that we're breaking the pattern of mourning.

At that moment I knew that Melissa and I had to get away to someplace where we could laugh when we wanted and cry when we wanted without being told that we weren't following the mourner's manual. And so we took a long vacation in Greece, where no one knew us; and there we felt suspended from our grief and almost outside it. We were getting ready for what we knew would be the hardest adjustment of our lives, for living without the third member of our tightly knit team.

When we returned, however, we still weren't ready for the different ways that each of us would make the adjustment while facing our grief. Back at the University of Pennsylvania, Melissa began to criticize me constantly. She couldn't understand that I had to be busy all the time to maintain my sanity, something I hadn't always taken good care of. After twenty-two years of marriage,

I was desperately lonely in a big empty house; and so, when anyone asked me to go out, I always said yes. Anything to get away from the now soundless bedroom. I was the first to arrive at parties and the last to leave. I was rebounding as furiously as Dennis Rodman.

When a single man I knew invited me and Melissa to have Thanksgiving with him, our first without Edgar, I gladly accepted, but Melissa exploded.

"If we're not having dinner at home, I'm not coming!" she cried. "We belong at *home*, in California. Daddy's body isn't even cold. Mother, how could you plan a holiday with some other man! How *could* you?!"

The conversation almost ended with a slammed-down phone, but I never do that. As irritated as I was with Melissa that fall and winter, I never hung up the phone without telling her that I loved her. Our gender and ages made things even harder. To a mother a teenage daughter is a member of a different species, one that does not communicate well with human beings.

At last, one February day, I went to Philadelphia for a joint therapy session with Melissa; we had been arguing for two solid weeks. And she did her best: For most of an hour she screamed at me, until the therapist finally said, "Melissa, give your mother a break. She's trying to reach out to you."

And suddenly the venting was over and both of us felt better. When I began to cry, Melissa saw at last that I also had been struggling with Edgar's death, that I also had been in pain, that I also had been trying to cope as well as I could.

Melissa warmed up at once; but now I was the one too hurt and angry to reconcile.

"Let's have a cup of coffee," she said.

"No, I can't talk to you now," I replied. "I have to go back to New York."

For several months after that, whenever we went out, we invited a friend so that we wouldn't be alone. I let Melissa know that I loved her, but revealed no details of my private life for her to criticize or judge. And then, little by little, we found our way back to each other, two veterans who had been through the same war but on different fronts. No matter how much you love someone, you must decide what you can give them and where you have to draw the line to conserve your strength.

"I'm slowly learning how often I can visit my dad in the nursing home," says a woman named Sandra, whose father has Alzheimer's, "and when it becomes destructive to my own life. Sometimes I just have to say 'enough' and put myself first — before my husband, before the kids."

Taking care of your own needs sometimes means conserving not only your time and energy but your money too.

"After the hurricane," says Karen, "a lot of people put their insurance money into replacing their kids' things — all the toys and all the clothes. But for way too long I'd been putting my kids ahead of myself in ways they didn't appreciate. You think a five-year-old boy cares if he wore the same shirt last Thursday? Of course I wanted my kids to have clean clothes and enough toys, but I knew they could get along with a lot less than they had; and I knew that I, who hadn't bought clothes since my divorce, deserved to take better care of myself."

Karen was taking a chance on her kids one day appearing on a talk show with the theme "Children of Mothers Who Sometimes Thought of Themselves."

Not matter how you cope, you're bound to get some bad reviews. In spite of our talk about rugged individualism, Americans still prefer smooth conformists who behave in a "proper" way. Burying your husband? Wear black and don't smile for three months. Lost your business? Sell your BMW and start eating at Burger King. Maybe your husband loved you in that skimpy red dress, and you want to wear it to his funeral as a final sign of love. And maybe the BMW is a reminder of how you fought your way up to build the business you just lost; and driving it may be the best reminder that you have what it takes to make it to the top again.

Never let others bully you out of your own particular style. I heard of one middle-aged woman who said to her mother, "Why are you still setting the table for Dad? He's been dead for six months."

No, that mother wasn't auditioning for a part in *Looney Tunes*. She was simply being true to herself and doing something that made her feel better.

After Edgar's death I ignored considerable advice, much of it from my financial advisers.

"Sell everything," they said, "and retire."

But I had never listened to critics who said the same thing. I have always taken great pride in my work and the way I built my career in spite of early criticism and rejection. And so, being surrounded by proof of my success was vital to me at a time when my husband was dead and my career on life support.

When I finally convinced my accountants that somehow I would find a way to pay my bills, I thought I'd be free to grieve as I wanted to. But friends continued to tell me the right way to mourn and for how long, the reasons I should or shouldn't date, and the reasons I should or shouldn't go back to work. Instinctively, however, I knew the wisdom of what Mariette Hartley had said to Melissa and me: There was no officially right way to handle things.

For example, people said I should stay close to home. Well, I moved to New York. And they also said not to make any major change in myself during the painful transition. Well, I put my hairdresser and Barney's on speed dial. I vowed to listen to myself at all times, for I had learned that people who listen to their inner voices usually bounce back faster and stronger than those who are meek and obedient.

One such person is my friend Ian.

Like Frank Sinatra, Ian can say, "I did it *my* way." When his magazine business suddenly failed, Ian was left with just two thousand dollars in the bank and ten times that much in debt. All his friends told him to declare bankruptcy.

Instead, he withdrew the last of his savings, flew to the Bahamas, and lay on the beach for a week.

By the time he got home, he was rested and thinking clearly. He managed to find a buyer for his business, paid off his debts, and had enough left to start a new magazine — all because he ignored every bit of advice except what came from inside.

Two months after Edgar's death, Melissa and I honored our instincts in a memorable way. We were in New York to attend Yom Kippur services at Emanu-El, the biggest Reform Jewish temple in North America. This was going to be Melissa's first time to say Kaddish — the prayer for the dead — for her father. The service was to start at three o'clock, but because we'd been stuck in a heavy rain, we arrived fifteen minutes late.

At my synagogue in Los Angeles, a three-o'clock Yom Kippur meant three-thirty or maybe five.

"Is Madonna here yet?"

"Wait — Whitney Houston is coming to say the *barucha*."

At the front door now, the usher looked at our tickets and told us we couldn't come in because we were late and there were no more seats. In a temple that size, there had to be seats, but the usher wanted to show us that he wouldn't bend the rules for a celebrity. And so, with tears in our eyes, Melissa and I stood in the rain outside the temple from which we were barred because of a policy that was an ecclesiastical version of Lincoln Center's no one seated during the first act. And Yom Kippur was a one-acter.

Melissa looked so lost, so forlorn, standing there in the rain on her first religious holiday without her father.

The hell with the rules of spending the day praying and fasting, I thought, and I took her around the corner to Ralph Lauren; at least he was Jewish. When we entered, a salesperson brought us wine. And there, in that temple of fashion, on the day when our religion said that we were to look into our souls, we drank Chablis and looked into three-way mirrors. I felt that God would understand, especially when he saw Melissa smiling again.

No two people comfort themselves in the same way.

"After my brother got sick," says a woman named Lisa, "he turned into Daddy Warbucks: He gave away a ton of money to strangers, leaving huge tips in restaurants, giving Christmas presents to people he barely knew. When I asked him why, he said he liked to imagine all those random people, many of them cynics, getting these surprise windfalls for no reason and deciding that the world might not be such a bad place after all."

"After my mom died," says a man named Al, "I was so deep in grief that I knew I had to do something to take me out of myself. My life was in pieces: I'd just been fired and my girlfriend had just thrown me out of our apartment in Venice Beach, California. I needed a real fantasy escape. So I started dressing up in spangled gowns and high heels and going down the Venice boardwalk. It made me laugh when nothing else did. It worked for me."

That route may be a bit way out for most of us, but it worked for him and that's what's important.

What is going to make *you* feel better?

Start by making a list of everything you feel tempted to do — *everything,* short of tax fraud or robbing a grave. Now go through the list and cross out anything that might put you in a police lineup. Look at what's left: going dancing while you're supposed to be in mourning; telling off your ex-mother-in-law; taking a leave of absence from your job and house swapping with a family in Tahiti or Buffalo.

Just remember: There are no rules. Whatever you do to work your way through your grief doesn't have to make sense.

"After my husband died," says a woman named Sheila, "I realized there were two things I never had done: take a vacation on my own and sleep with someone other than my husband. So I booked a flight to Paris and actually bought condoms in a drugstore.

"Well, when I got to Paris," says Sheila, "with my little carry-on condoms, the idea of sleeping with a stranger was less enticing; I still had fifties values about sex, love, and marriage. However, I realized that I didn't have to sleep with strangers to have the thrill of being a single woman on the loose. So I flirted with men and had drinks with them and even let one kiss me passionately on a bridge over the Seine. When I came home, people said I looked wonderful, but I told them nothing of what I did. I didn't feel like being judged about what a widow my age is supposed to do."

Sheila was smart: People are particularly critical of widows. At one of my lectures, a woman told the audience that, after her husband's death, people told her unsmilingly that she looked marvelous, as if looking marvelous were an insult to her husband's memory.

And then this woman told us, to great applause, that her standard response was "Why *shouldn't* I look good? I'm not the one who died."

Whatever you do to recover from a loss,

people will be critical because they believe that the only way to recover is *their* way. And you will even run into some people who should be run into by rhinos because they actually don't want to see you get over your tragedy at all; grief is a spectator sport for them.

About four months after Edgar died, I was in a coffee shop with friends and one of them cracked a good joke. I laughed hard. And then a complete stranger came over and said, one slow cold word at a time, "I. Knew. Your. Husband," and walked away.

She was, of course, an *in*complete stranger: Brains were missing in this woman who thought it was inappropriate for me to be doing anything but weeping in solitary confinement.

In difficult times pamper yourself; do whatever makes you feel better. Don't stop getting manicures just because you lost your job. In fact, *this* is the time for your hands to look beautiful. The man of your dreams may work in the unemployment office.

"I've definitely learned that it's okay to spoil myself in little ways," says Mindy. "Every few months, my husband and I leave the baby with my in-laws for the weekend and check into a motel. I know couples who never do that, who say they'll wait till the summer or till the kids are older. Well, my mother's death taught me you never know how much time you have. The years pass too quickly. I've learned it's important to indulge myself."

As William Saroyan said, "In the time of your life, live."

5

AND THE MOON AT NIGHT

After a tragedy, a loss, a blow of any kind, your mission is simply to get unstuck. It is *always* a "mission possible"; defeat is not an option for you. The game isn't over till the fat lady sings, but *your* fat lady has laryngitis.

A glowing example: In the summer of 1984, a young woman named Vanessa Williams became the first African-American Miss America. A few months later, when the pageant's director learned that a magazine had published nude photos of her, Vanessa Williams became the first Miss America of any color to be stripped of her crown. The woman was subjected to unique national humiliation.

Well, Vanessa may have lost her crown, but she didn't lose her head — or heart. Conventional wisdom said that the disgrace of the scandal meant she was finished. Her next career move would be a booking at the Pasadena Auto Show.

And conventional wisdom was wrong. Vanessa, whose voice was as good as her figure, fought her way back into show business and began to record songs. When her recording of "The Right Stuff" became the first of her many big hits, it was pretty clear that Vanessa Williams had also displayed naked spunk.

And so, no matter how trapped in the Krazy Glue of life you may be feeling, you *can* get unstuck. My favorite way is to make a list of all that I have to be thankful for. It's a particularly good way to end the day, as Irving Berlin told us when he wrote, "And I fall asleep counting my blessings."

So now it is time to put away your self-pity list and make a much sunnier one: Write down everything that makes you feel good — for example, this book. If you're having trouble getting started, look again to Irving Berlin, who told us how lucky we are to have the sun in the morning and the moon at night — except in Lapland, of course, where they have the sun in the morning *and* the sun at night — and the grass. And the fact that you can see it in a world where so many people are blind.

Your gratitude list will get you unstuck and also leave you feeling optimistic about your future.

"After a death," says psychologist Janis Heil, "people often get stuck because they think they need to hold on to the pain in order to retain the memories. Feeling guilty for moving on, they say, 'How can I even think of going ahead with my life when the person I loved is gone?' "

"And sometimes," says therapist Amy

Bloom, "we cling because the memory is so painful that we can't stop visiting it and hoping to make it come out differently. The risk of letting go is that we have to confront our own selves and our own possibilities."

In May 1995, on the twenty-fifth anniversary of the shootings at Kent State, I heard a radio interview with a woman who had seen that horror.

"It stopped my life forever," she said.

Lady, I thought, you are a fool. Think of all you could have done in twenty-five years to keep tragedies like that from happening again. Has living in the seventies brought those victims back to life?

And as for you, sitting in the same chair for seven years isn't going to bring your loved one back. It will merely bring you one bad back. At the end of our lives, we get no bonus for time spent feeling sorry for ourselves. Saint Peter won't be greeting me with a coupon that says: Good for five pounds of nectar to make up for the time you spent crying after *Sally Marr* closed.

Self-pity shortens your life: Studies have shown that all down emotions can lead to illness: Pessimism should come with a warning from the surgeon general. No matter how distraught I feel, I always draw the line between sadness, which is a natural part of life, and self-pity, which immobilizes you.

The first thing I do is to start moving physically. I get dressed for business and put my makeup on.

"Put a little lipstick on, darling, you'll feel better," your grandmother probably used to say.

Well, she was right: The Cosmetics, Fragrance, and Toiletries Foundation has done research that proved that caring for your appearance can both boost your health and relieve depression. And so, even if you're going to be home alone, put on makeup, stockings, and jewelry, particularly if you're a woman. Just getting dressed is a signal to yourself that you are ready to resume living.

Let me tell you how wonderful the will to survive can be, whether conscious or visceral. Let me tell you how magnificently a human being can move on, no matter what misfortune he or she is moving out of.

The 1996 triple Grammy winner was a thirty-three-year-old singer-composer named Seal. Okay, so his name is not exactly Mel Torme. It could have been worse: He could have been called Herring.

But the right name for Seal is Guts.

Do you know what this triple Grammy winner bounced back from? The triple crown of bad luck: childhood abandonment, abuse, and disease. When he was six, his mother was deported and he was sent to live with his father, where life wasn't exactly *Father Knows Best.* Father's hobby was beating Seal with whips, belts, and fists. He wanted the boy to be a doctor. When Seal started singing, his father beat him even more.

As if life hadn't already given Seal enough blows, when he was twenty-three, he came down with lupus, which scarred his face and threatened his life with a generally incurable disease.

But this young man simply refused to let anything stop him.

"I was always able to see the light at the end of the tunnel," says Seal, whose triumph over adversity has been a definite example of the fruits of optimism. To the pessimist the light at the end of the tunnel is another train. Don't *you* take this view of life's railroad!

After a blow simply figure out what you have to do to survive. Having trouble staying away from drugs or alcohol? Then go to AA or other twelve-step meetings. Do you or a loved one have a serious illness? Make a list of the doctors or treatments you need and schedule them at once. Need to pay the mortgage but your husband ran off with all your money? Call a lawyer; and if you can't afford one, call Legal Aid. In the meantime, if you can, borrow some money from a relative or a friend.

Need to get the kids back in school after the death of their father? Need to find a job? Check the want ads, see headhunters, and call everyone you know. Network like mad: Personal contacts are supremely important. According to one Chicago placement firm, 40 percent of all jobs are landed through personal contacts. How do you think Hillary Clinton got the health care gig?

Ask *everyone*, and follow up on *every* lead. Keep saying, "Do you know anyone who might be looking for a receptionist?" — or a teacher, a librarian, or a crop duster? Be flexible, ready to compromise, ready to take a pay cut to get started in a new career. What are your greatest assets? Well, you certainly know how to stay calm in a crisis.

The ability to adapt to new conditions is the key: Forget everything you've ever heard about what's "proper" and what's "suitable" for you. Be willing to see yourself in a new light, the way Charlie Pride did.

Today we know Charlie Pride as one of the greatest country-and-western singers of all time. He has thirty-nine gold albums, two platinum ones, and one quadruple platinum. He has won three Grammys and has twice been the Country Music Association's Entertainer of the Year.

Not bad for an alternate career. You see, the humming that first enticed Charlie came from the baseball he pitched so well as a boy. At the age of sixteen, he was able to play on a minor league team.

In 1961 he tried out as a pitcher with the California Angels; but the Angels' manager told him that he didn't have a major league arm, so he was sent home. The next year he went for a tryout at the training camp of the New York Mets, which had just entered the National League as an expansion team. Again Charlie was rejected; and rejection by the '62 Mets, a team almost as good as the Bad News Bears, was like being told he wasn't handsome enough to play the Hunchback of Notre Dame.

Well, perhaps Charlie Pride didn't have a major league arm, but he happened to have a Hall of Fame heart.

"I decided," said Charlie, "to try something else."

Like another young pitcher, who once tried out for the Washington Senators but wasn't quite good enough. And so Fidel Castro tried something else.

As Helen Keller said: "Life is either a daring adventure or nothing."

6

CATCH A FALLING STAR

You probably know much more than you give yourself credit for, and your ability to learn is greater than you think. After Edgar's death I was suddenly aware of great gaps in my knowledge. For example, I didn't know how to balance a checkbook. Balance it? I didn't know where it *was*.

However, I had always been a fast learner, so I enrolled in Accounting 101 at UCLA. In my notebook I put the kind of financial facts you never get from Alan Greenspan:

This is a picture of a deposit slip. They're in the top left drawer.

This is a picture of a withdrawal slip. It takes money *out* of the bank — if you have any there.

There were many other facets to my ignorance. I didn't know how to program the VCR, something the average eight-year-old can do as if tying her shoes. I couldn't even start the car, because Edgar had gotten a German model and you needed a month at Berlitz to read the dashboard. The only driving I was doing was driving myself crazy over being unemployed.

Luckily, despite big cash-flow problems after Edgar's death, I had enough money not to end up homeless or hungry. Nevertheless, I needed to start working again, not only to stay solvent but sane. The self-esteem that came from my work had always been supremely important to me. And it was also supremely important not to sit at home and go mad wondering what I might have done to avert the tragedy.

At first I was terrified by the prospect of looking for work. Suppose I found nothing but a lively lack of interest in me? I was fifty-two years old and what they call a star. Was I supposed to look under *S* in the help-wanted ads? And then I remembered: Even though I had worked steadily for twenty-five years before my late-night show was canceled, I was no stranger to unemployment.

My first job, as a Barnard College student, had been guiding tours around Rockefeller Center. And I loved it: Talking to the public and showing them around was like acting in a small play. One night, however, I was given the late shift, and the tour on that shift consisted of just one man, who struck me as weird. Because I was nervous about his potential, I cut the tour down to about three minutes.

Unfortunately, my boss was not impressed

by my being able to give a tour that was the length of a station break. I was fired and rightfully so; but the blow was enormous. I had loved playing Radio City.

After college I got a job at an ad agency. Because I was also trying to launch my stand-up comedy career at the same time, I was getting about four hours of sleep every night. Being half awake was a painless though not particularly efficient way to check advertising copy. My supervisor had told me to put an initial over every word and picture to show I had proofread it.

One day, one of our clients, an airline, placed a full-page ad in the *New York Times* saying: "We Now Fly Cross Country Six Times a Day." The ad had a picture of six planes, but only eleven wings. What did they expect? I wasn't a math major; I was a tired English major, one who knew that she couldn't do *everything* well.

A few minutes after the ad appeared in print, my boss appeared at my desk to inform me that I was fired. What really annoyed him was that he had to wake me up to do so.

Each time I was fired, I thought: Well, now it's over for good. I'll never get another job.

Soon, however, I managed to return to Rockefeller Center in the publicity department of Radio City Music Hall. And there my creativity knew no bounds for a rerelease of *Snow White and the Seven Dwarfs.*

"I've got a great idea!" I said. "Let's get seven midgets, dress them up as the Seven Dwarfs, and put them out on the marquee to wave to the kids."

My boss loved the idea, and I suddenly saw myself running the publicity department by the time I was twenty-two.

Unfortunately, it was a bitter cold day, and my boss suggested that I send some hot coffee up to the midgets; but I decided to send them liquor instead. At once they seized the opportunity to get drunk, and began to shout remarks to the kids that never would have come from Disney. It took three security guards to bring them down.

Once again Joan was Dopey.

The incident made all the papers, and I was given another chance to savor unemployment. I felt devastated. Was there no way I could fit in? Was I too headstrong ever to hold a job?

And so, many years after lubricating those midgets, I was pondering Fox's cancellation of *The Late Show Starring Joan Rivers,* and I told myself that I could survive again the same way I always had: by swallowing my pride and moving to the bottom of the heap. I remembered the Chinese proverb: The glory is not in never failing, but in rising every time you fail.

I have always felt that life is like a magical paneled room: You hit every panel until one swings open and you realize it's a door — a small door, of course, but one nonetheless. With this room in mind, I took out my Rolodex and started calling people: ones who knew me, ones who didn't know me, and ones who didn't like me. I summoned my courage to call the second group and swallowed my pride to call the third. I told anyone who would listen that I was willing to work anywhere at any time, as long as I could perform to make people laugh.

My friends began the laughing when they heard that I had finally been able to get myself on *Hollywood Squares*, not the memorable old one but a new struggling one, whose host was John Davidson. John would walk out onstage, say "Hello, stars," and they would all look around to see who the hell he was talking to. The show had guests who'd almost been on *M*A*S*H* and people whose careers had peaked with guest appearances on *The Love Boat*.

When the producers asked me if I would like to be the center square, I thought it over for two or three seconds and said yes. On taping days I would drive to the Fox lot and make up in my old dressing room because life is run by the gods of absurdity. And the man at the gate would say, "Boy, do we miss you," and I'd smile with pride in my throat. Six months before, I'd been queen of this lot; and now I was one of nine squares in a syndicated and marginal show. At least no one put a spotlight on me, as a technician had done to Norma Desmond in *Sunset Boulevard*, and said, "Hey, Miss Rivers! It's Hawkeye! Let's have a look at you!"

When you are going through a crisis, you check your ego at the door. Hell, even when things are going *well* in show business — or *any* business — the door is the place for your ego to be.

The year after Judy Holliday had won a Tony for being the best actress in a musical, for being the incandescent star of *The Bells Are Ringing*, she was interested in starring in a new show, whose producer said she had to audition for it.

"Absolutely not!" said her lover, jazz great Gerry Mulligan. "You don't audition! You're *Judy Holliday!*"

"Oh well," said Judy. "It's only humiliation."

And so, in finding a new job, a new home, new friends, or whatever you're going for, thoughts of embarrassment, humiliation, or even mortification simply have no place. With merry chutzpah, just keep going forward.

After my jewelry business was dragged into the Regal Communications bankruptcy, I knew I'd be needing the best bankruptcy lawyers. No one I knew had ever gone bankrupt (except morally), so I could ask none of my friends to suggest a lawyer. Therefore I followed a Joan Rivers rule: Whenever possible, go to the top. I called the brilliant financier Donald Trump, whom I'd met just once at a dinner party. Knowing he was probably too busy to take my call, I told his secretary, "I'm in a huge mess, I don't know what to do, and I need his recommendation of the best bankruptcy lawyers. I'd be grateful if you could get back to me with a name."

The following day she called back with a name. Was it worth prostrating myself before a perfect stranger? Yes, and before an imperfect one too. The lawyer Trump recommended eventually got me my business back. To survive you've got to be willing to swallow your pride and ask for help.

And, while swallowing and asking, you've got to figure out every survival skill you have. One of mine happens to be short-term leadership. (My attention span wouldn't have let me spend forty years leading the

Jews out of Egypt.) I'm the woman you want in charge when the elevator breaks down and the alarm isn't working and someone has to organize people to keep their cool for an hour or so.

Pretending that my life was a broken-down elevator — and I didn't have to pretend very hard — I got on the phone at once and called the lawyers Trump had recommended. Acting quickly made it easier for me to respond to the enraged debtors and to begin the long process of getting my business back.

What are *your* greatest skills and strengths? If you made a list of them for job hunting a few pages back, return to that list and keep writing. You'll be surprised how many you have.

And let me repeat, keep listening *only* to yourself. The headmaster of an English boys' school once said to a student who had performed in a school play: "I'll tell you one thing, Guinness: You're no actor." Fortunately for the world, that student kept listening only to Alec Guinness.

Oh, you can listen to Calvin Coolidge, too. In his lifetime Coolidge didn't say much. In fact, when informed of his death, Dorothy Parker said, "How can they tell?" But Coolidge did have one moment, and it produced these memorable words: "Press on.

Nothing in the world can take the place of persistence. Talent will not: nothing is more common than unrewarded talent. Education alone will not: the world is full of educated failures. Persistence alone is omnipotent."

When I first tried to break into show business, I got rejection after rejection; and from the people who should have been supporting me, I got only discouraging words.

"You have no talent," one woman said. "You're throwing your life away."

And that woman was my mother!

One of the biggest theatrical agents told me, "You've been around too long. Everyone who could help you in our business has seen you. If you were going to make it, you would have made it by now."

I went to audition for the *Tonight Show* seven times — *seven times* — and at the end of the seventh audition, the talent coordinator said, "We just don't think you'd work on TV."

I had no money. My office was a phone booth in Grand Central Station. I lived out of one small suitcase and slept in my car. My family thought I'd gone crazy, and my father threatened to have me committed to Bellevue. (It would have been the only booking I could get.) The verdict certainly seemed to be in, but I just couldn't quit. Perhaps I knew instinctively how thunderingly wrong early verdicts can be.

For example: There was once a Broadway performer named Fred Astaire who went to Hollywood for a screen test. And this is what one studio executive wrote after seeing Astaire's test: "Not handsome, can't act, dances a little."

Deep inside me, I must have known that I could be funny a little.

Phyllis Diller knew it too — that *she* could be funny, I mean. Listen to all the reasons that Phyllis had to quit.

"Shortly after I got my first job as a night club comic," she says, "the management changed and I was fired. Then I was booked to do a sketch on *The Steve Allen Show*. After three days of rehearsal I was fired. Then I signed with a new agency that sent me to the hottest spot in Miami Beach, the Fontainbleau Hotel. After the first show, I was fired. Then I was fired by the agency."

But, like me, Phyllis never gave up. Like me, she believed in herself. It didn't matter that the two of us were fired from everything but a cannon. (I wonder if either of us would have done that for laughs.)

And so, if you forget everything else I'm telling you — and you'd better not — remember this: In every human endeavor, persistence is everything.

You may have heard of a book by Mary Pipher called *Reviving Ophelia: Saving the Selves of Adolescent Girls*. It was on the *New York Times* bestseller list for almost two years. A natural for any smart publisher to grab, right? Well, the first thirteen publishers to which Mary Pipher submitted this book rejected it. At that point it might have been a case of reviving Mary, but she never weakened and the fourteenth publisher accepted it.

Composer Meredith Willson needed even more optimism than Mary Pipher. In the mid-1950s he wrote a joyous musical that brought no joy to almost every producer in New York: about forty of them rejected it. At last Willson found one who liked it. And that's how America was given *The Music Man*.

Do you know how America got Dr. Seuss, its most beloved children's book author? Because Seuss, whose real name was Ted Geisel, was more cheerfully persistent than the Cat in the Hat. In 1937 he wrote his first book, *And to Think That I Saw It on Mulberry Street*. It was rejected by thirty-seven publishers before the thirty-eighth accepted it. Thirty-seven publishers had been as dumb as the Grinch, but they hadn't stopped Ted Geisel.

And look at Alexander Graham Bell, who did *twenty-two thousand* experiments before he hit on the telephone. Just a few more and he would have had call waiting.

The man I plan to marry, Orin Lehman, makes Pipher, Willson, and Bell seem like pessimists: At the age of seventy-four, he likes to play golf. Yes, of course, many men of seventy-four play golf; but how many of them lost a leg in Germany in World War II?

When other golfers ask Orin, "What's your handicap?" I can hear him wanting to reply, "Absolutely none."

And so, *never* worry about the odds against you. Didn't General Custer say that? Well, he did give it a shot. And he got more than one back.

Of *course* there are times when you're going to lose; but you *have* to stay at the table; you have to keep playing the game. Teddy Roosevelt put it eloquently:

The credit belongs to the man who is actually in the arena; whose face is marred by dust and sweat and blood; who strives valiantly; who errs and comes short again and again; who knows the great enthusiasms . . . and if he fails, at least fails while daring greatly; so that his place will never be with those cold and timid souls who know neither victory nor defeat.

7

WITH A LITTLE HELP FROM YOUR FRIENDS

In the business of survival, one of your greatest strengths is friends. Don't be too proud to ask them for help. I was truly lucky to have had so many friends respond when I called them for comfort after Edgar's suicide, friends like Coral Browne, the English actress and wife of Vincent Price. Always elegantly groomed, Coral drove to my house in her bathrobe the moment she heard the news. There she was, half naked and uncoiffed, offering her love, oblivious to the way she was dressed.

Dorothy Melvin, my wondrous manager, left a romantic tryst with a new lover and flew back to be with me. Tommy Corcoran, for years Carol Burnett's manager and my friend since my days as a struggling young comic, flew from New York for Edgar's funeral in such haste that he brought no baggage. And there was Kenneth Battelle, the legendary hairdresser, who never broke appointments; but he broke dozens to fly to me. And there was Ann Pierce, my close friend and dresser, who flew from Texas and literally slept in my bed for a few nights. When I got up to cry at four in the morning, she was there to hold my hand.

Overriding my pride was my instinct to

survive, which told me that it was okay to accept all this help. Help also went to Melissa and touched her deeply. At her college, the *Daily Pennsylvanian* had run a big story about the suicide. Moments after the paper came out, two of her friends walked all over the campus and removed the paper from the lobby of every building she usually entered so she wouldn't see it.

Often people who can't think of specific ways to help you will be able to help with just a touch or a smile.

"A lot of people, ones I expected nothing from," says Melissa, "would just randomly come up and hug me and then walk away. It was very moving."

Melissa and I learned that, no matter how alone you feel in the face of tragedy, there are good people around who want to help you. Watch the TV news after a disaster and you'll see the kind of goodness I'm talking about. You'll see the way volunteers from all over the country went to Oklahoma City to help devastated families after the bombing or traveled to Los Angeles after the earthquake just so they could help in any way.

"When my daughter was killed by a drunk driver," says a woman named Lorreine, "I realized that the only way anyone was going to know what happened was if I *let* them know. My family and friends are spread out all over the country. I had to figure out which people to call and which people could call *others*, so I didn't have to repeat the horrible story over and over again."

Even supportive friends may withdraw that support after a while: If you don't keep asking for help, they may assume you're okay. Or they may feel that showing too much concern will be taken as a sign that they think you're in deep trouble. Or they may not know what the hell to think because people aren't always Salvation Army generals; they're sometimes Beetle Baileys.

Often people simply do not listen to what you're saying. You'll meet a friend on the street and she'll say, "How are you?"

"I just found out that I have six weeks to live," you'll reply.

"That's nice. And the family?"

"My son was lost on a Boy Scout hike, and my daughter fell into a volcano."

"Glad to hear it. Have a good day."

If you aren't getting the support you need, speak up and spell things out for both friends and acquaintances. Eager to return to their own lives after helping you, your friends can lose track of your continuing pain, especially after a formal period of mourning. Don't be shy about working updates on how you're feeling into conversations.

"I had always been very independent," says a woman named Debra. "I'm a marathon runner, and I run my own business. But after my husband was killed in a plane crash, I realized that no one gets through a tragedy like that alone. After a lifetime of telling everyone, 'I don't need any help, thanks,' I knew I needed to change my attitude. So I started calling people to say, 'I need a friend. Can you come over and keep me company tonight after the kids go to sleep?' Most of them said yes."

After *Sally Marr* closed and my business was gone, my casual acquaintances didn't keep coming by the way they had after Edgar's suicide — not because they didn't care but because they were unaware of what I was going through. They didn't know that I was not just in debt but in deep pain.

"The best way to ask for support," says Dr. Susan Bodnar, "is in little doses. Don't tell a friend, 'Help, I'm falling apart!' She'll be overwhelmed. Instead say, 'I opened Jim's medicine cabinet this morning and his aftershave made me so sad. Can you come over for a cup of coffee so I can talk about it?' "

"My friend's husband abandoned her a year before my own left me," says Betty. "She'd found a great lawyer. So I asked her out to lunch and not only got the lawyer's name but also other tips so I wouldn't get screwed in court by my ex-husband."

Sometimes the best thing a friend can offer you is just a slightly different perspective, particularly if the friend is a man.

Says Meghan, "One guy told me, 'It's really cool you're getting divorced. It shows you've gone for something and don't always play it safe.' That boosted my confidence a lot."

I wonder if some guy told Elizabeth Taylor: "It's really cool you get divorced every year they have the Olympics."

Be realistic about what each person can and can't offer you. And then make simple, direct requests, like this: "My mother is sick and I have to spend every day at the hospital. Do you have any spare time to take my kids out for ice cream?"

Of course, even when you're clear about your needs, people sometimes won't come through for you because of their own needs or feelings. Edgar's best friend, Tom Pileggi, didn't come to the memorial service, and I understood and accepted his reason. Edgar had promised Tom that he wouldn't do anything foolish and Tom had replied, "If you do, I won't come to your funeral." I had to respect Tom being a man of his word.

There are times when a loss is compounded by a feeling of isolation, especially if you moved to a new town just before the tragedy hit and haven't made many friends.

"My husband and I had just retired to Boca Raton when he had a massive stroke," says Sheila. "We had only a stick-shift car that I didn't know how to drive, so I couldn't get to the hospital. I had to knock on the doors of acquaintances and say, 'Hello, nice to meet you. Could you be my chauffeur?' "

When I hit bottom, I felt like telling people, "Hello, nice to meet you. Could you reunite me with my daughter, find me a new business, and produce a new television show for me — not necessarily in that order?"

However, I shouldn't say "when I hit bottom" because I never saw it as that. After the loss of my Edgar, my business, and my show, I often remembered the words of another Edgar, the one in *King Lear*: "The worst is not, so long as we can say 'This is the worst.' "

In other words, if you are still alive, stop your bitching. Shakespeare was one smart cookie.

Once you find people who are willing to help you, be selective. Find upbeat people, not those who enjoy wallowing in their own misery. Avoid any daughters of Queen Victoria — any women whose favorite outfit is widow's weeds.

"After my own divorce," says psychologist Julia Daniels, "many depressed women wanted me to do things with them in the evening. They were drawn to another person in crisis; but they wanted only to *dwell* on their problems, not solve them. Luckily I knew enough to stay away from people who weren't doing anything to get through their own depression."

And so, stick with the optimists, who know, as Florence Henderson does, that "just when you think nothing good can come out of a situation, that's when something wonderful happens."

In 1954, after touring all over the United States for a year as Laurey in *Oklahoma!*, Florence took a screen test for this very role in the movie version of *Oklahoma!* But she didn't get the part and she was devastated.

"I guess I cried a little," she says, "but I didn't give up. I went back on the road for another year of *Oklahoma!* and learned more in that year than in any other. And because I'd learned so much, Josh Logan called me to audition for a new Broadway musical called *Fanny.* I got the part and suddenly found myself on Broadway, singing opposite Ezio Pinza."

Florence Henderson didn't need to hear Calvin Coolidge: She knew instinctively that nothing was more important than perseverance.

"When I first started appearing on the *Jack Paar Show*," she says, "my agent told me I was wrong, but my gut instinct told me the opposite, and I stuck to my guns. I've never felt like quitting. If I'm rejected for something, I always think that I'm being saved for something better. I always believe that everything works itself out to the positive."

Could there have been a better choice for the mother of *The Brady Bunch*? Except for me, of course. I always sing while putting out the doilies.

And so, as Johnny Mercer wrote: "Accentuate the positive, eliminate the negative."

A negative attitude is literally contagious. Psychologists at the University of Texas studied ninety-six pairs of college roommates and discovered that when one was depressed, the other caught that depression in about three weeks.

Completely eliminate negative people from your life, and pursue only the upbeat. And among these upbeat, pick the ones with brains, not the ones who think an evening's entertainment is trashing your ex-husband, the very man you want to forget. And not the ones who think that the solution to your problem is shopping till you drop — not the ideal solution if your problem is bankruptcy.

And don't accept help from anyone whose motives you distrust. Believe it or not, there are actually people who don't have your best interests at heart.

"I had one acquaintance," says Melissa, "who was a compulsive liar. She seemed as though she was really coming through for me. However, she was running around telling everybody what she did for me, mostly things she hadn't done. She was using her tales of saving me to make herself look good."

Of course, the person doing the most to make Melissa look good was Melissa. Her bouncing back made me think of what Molière said: "The greater the obstacle, the more glory in overcoming it."

8

THINK SHRINK

Of all the help you can get, perhaps none is more important than that of a therapist. From my own experience and from the stories of men and women all over the country, I have learned that some problems are simply too complex to be solved by anyone but a good therapist.

Just before Edgar's funeral, a friend of mine gave me the name of a psychologist and said, "Joan, I really think you ought to talk to a professional."

The owners of comedy clubs used to tell me the same thing.

Although a therapist had helped Melissa and me to resolve some standard mother-daughter tension a few years earlier, I wondered now if a psychologist could help me with my much deeper problem. But I found that one could; for there is nothing like discussing your troubles with a trained and objective outsider, someone who carries no emotional baggage and can listen to you without judging.

"Psychologists can listen to things nobody else can handle," says Susan Bodnar. "We're trained to hear really intense feeling."

When a friend of yours hears really intense feeling, she may be uncomfortable and want to change the subject to liposuction. And in therapy you don't have to apologize for your feelings or interrupt them to say, "Well, enough about me. Doctor, how has *your* week been?"

With friends, no matter how supportive they are, there comes a time when you feel guilty about asking advice and taking their time. No guilt, of course, need be felt with a therapist: It's her *job* to help you.

And one more thing a therapist gives you: confidentiality. It's fine to have friends, but vows of silence aren't part of the human makeup. Confess to a friend, and you're liable to hear it played back to you by a beautician — and it won't even be exactly right.

"I hear you had a lovely weekend with a volleyball team at a Holiday Inn," she'll say, not knowing it was the Marriott.

But a therapist is ethically bound to keep your secrets, so you can tell him or her anything.

A therapist can also tell you what parts of your behavior are a reaction to your loss and what parts are the fundamental mess that's you. Are you throwing that bottle at your sister because of what you've just been through or because you want to remind her that she's always been a bitch? A therapist will let you see how your current pain is affecting your behavior and what old wounds still need to be healed.

"I saw my counselor for about three years," says Karen, "much longer than I'd planned. I figured I just needed a few sessions to talk about how helpless the hurricane made me feel. But once I started talking, the hurricane brought up all kinds of unresolved feelings, like the fact that moving around so much as a kid had been painful for me, and how my divorce had made me put so much pressure on myself to be the perfect mom."

Your therapy may, like Karen's, last longer than you anticipate; but you also may find that you need to see your therapist fewer times than you anticipated.

"About a year after my husband was killed in the plane crash," says Debra, "I went to a therapist because I thought there was something wrong with me for feeling so sad for so long. The doctor told me it was perfectly normal to feel sad for months or even years after someone dies — as long as those feelings don't hurt other relationships or keep you from enjoying other parts of your life."

Strict Freudian analysts are most interested in probing your childhood and dredging up memories that can unlock neuroses.

They want to know how I *felt* about being unpopular with boys. (I felt *wonderful,* doctor. Purity was important to me.) Freudian analysis, however, is usually wrong for coping with specific crises. If your husband just died or your child needs brain surgery, it wouldn't matter if you had been Rebecca of Sunnybrook Farm.

Besides Freudian therapy, there are many other kinds, such as Rogerian, rational-emotive, cognitive, and behavioral. One of them is bound to work for you. Whatever kind you're seeking, shop carefully. What kind of training does he or she have?

I was lucky: The first therapist I went to in Beverly Hills, Michael Greenstein, was a perfect fit for me. At once he understood my situation, and at once I felt comfortable with him. However, even when you do click with a therapist, you'll still need a few sessions before he understands the tapestry of your life, before you can tell him, "so then Dorothy said . . ." and have him know what that means. In script-writing, we call this back story. And when you're fifty-two years old, the back story covers a good chunk of American history.

No matter how good your psychologist is, your sessions will do you good only if you're completely honest. Edgar had deceived his psychiatrist: After the suicide this man told me he couldn't believe that Edgar had been unhappy. All they had ever talked about was foreign policy and books.

It took me a while to open up and tell Michael Greenstein everything. And one of those things was that, after Edgar's suicide, I became a bulimic.

A devastating loss can affect a person's appetite in two ways: either kill it or send it into orbit. For me the suicide inspired a gastronomic space program: I ate cookies by the bagful and ice cream by the pint. My lunches were huge, and my dinners were French, at fine restaurants almost every night of the week.

After a few weeks of trying to redefine overeating, I felt bloated and uncomfortable and my clothes all felt like rubber bands. Rather than say goodbye to my entire wardrobe, however, I came up with a solution, one that also might have occurred to a village idiot. I stuck my finger down my throat to make myself throw up; within minutes, my stomach was flat again. This was a popular pastime for the Romans, but Jews generally preferred gin rummy.

At first I allowed myself this treat just one night a week, after an especially big dinner. But soon I was doing it twice a week, then every night, then twice a day. I figured out that the best time to make myself throw up was exactly thirty minutes after I'd finished eating. Such precise recycling of my meal wasn't easy: While glancing nervously at my watch, I had to stretch the dinner conversation so I would still be at the restaurant a half hour later; *or* I had to rush the eating so I could be home in my own bathroom for the magic moment.

For some reason I never bothered to mention to my therapist this little trick I was doing with my intestines: putting them in reverse twice a day. I told myself that it was just "a little diet plan" — a disgusting one, of course, but one not relevant to my recovery. Exactly how would I have put it? "By the way, doctor, my finger isn't just for reading the wind and calling cabs. Two or three times a day, I stick it down my throat."

And there was one more consideration: I didn't want to stop throwing up, at least not yet.

There came a point, however, when I could no longer hide the truth, either from myself or Michael. One afternoon I was in a limousine on my way from New York to Atlantic City. Suddenly realizing that it was a half hour after I'd finished lunch, I told the driver to pull over to the next rest stop.

Dorothy Melvin, my manager, looked at me in shock, for she knew how fastidious I was: I once flew all the way to Rome without using the plane's bathroom; and even in the best hotel, I have to paper the toilet before I use it.

Yet there I was, asking to pull over to a highway rest stop. If you've ever been in one of those roadside bathrooms, you know that sticking your finger down your throat in one of them is redundant. Nevertheless I told Dorothy that I really had to relieve myself, but I wasn't truthful about the specific kind of relief. Moments later, as I threw up my lunch into a filthy toilet, I was wise enough to think, This is really sick.

I was being welcomed to rock bottom. It was time to tell Michael about my bulimia, but I was afraid he'd think I was certifiably crazy and beyond his power to help. At the same time I was also afraid that he'd force me to stop. How's *that* for being mixed up?! Michael, however, did what all good therapists do: He helped me to understand my behavior so I could change what had to be changed.

"Your life is out of control," he said. "You don't know where you're going, what you're doing, or who you are. The one thing you *can* control is what goes into your body and what comes out. At eight o'clock you can predict exactly what you'll be doing at half past: throwing up in the bathroom."

With Michael's help I learned to take control of not only my eating but also my life. When he died in 1993, I'd been having fewer and fewer sessions. Michael may have been gone, but my feeling for therapy was stronger than ever; and so, when I felt betrayed and alone after my bankruptcy and the closing of *Sally Marr*, I knew I had to find a New York psychologist at once. I was in a deep depression, despondent once again over the loss of my husband, my business, and my Broadway show, desperately worried about bankruptcy and desperately afraid of growing older all alone. For the first time in my life, I was possessed by despair.

I had big decisions to make and I didn't trust myself to make them; I needed the objectivity of a professional. First I had to decide if I should stay in New York or move back to Hollywood to rebuild my career. After all my setbacks, maybe I was ready to be a lounge act in Tijuana. Melissa hoped I'd move to California and live near her; but my New York friends couldn't understand why anyone would want to move to the "left coast."

This time, finding a therapist wasn't so

easy. The first one I saw said nothing but "Uh-huh . . . uh-huh" for forty-five minutes. Finally I asked him, "Aren't you going to say anything?"

"Aha!" he replied. "Why do you want me to say anything?"

Next came a man who stroked his beard and said, "This is going to be very interesting."

I didn't care if I was very boring. I wasn't there to be a class for him; I was there to figure out what to do with the rest of my life.

Shrink number three never smiled. The last thing I needed was a shrink who was a tough house. And the fourth one didn't stop laughing. He said he was a big fan of mine.

At last a friend recommended Dr. June Townsend. I went to see her, and we clicked. She perfectly understood my situation and my feelings. She helped me come to terms with the end of *Sally Marr*, and to decide what to do next with my life. With her help I admitted that I had never been happy in California since Edgar's death. Now my choice was to rebuild my show business career in California and be socially miserable or enjoy a good social life in New York, where rebuilding my career would be much harder.

For about a year I saw Dr. Townsend once

a week, until I felt strong and confident again. Since then I've seen her only once in a while, whenever I have to vent particularly strong feelings or get advice about my relationship with Melissa. If your own daughter or some other family member has created a problem for you, you may want to consider bringing other family members to therapy sessions so the therapist can see how all of you interact — if you're still speaking to one another. If not, he or she'll get you going.

In addition to the help of family counseling, you can also find help from various support groups. They exist for every situation you can imagine, from Parents of Murdered Children to Parents of People with AIDS. After Edgar's suicide I attended several such group sessions, and I learned perspective about the suffering of other people.

Into our survivors' group on a particularly bad day for me came a woman looking so marvelous that I wanted to kill either her or myself. She was a blue-eyed blond with a stunningly beautiful face, a model's body, and an outfit by Chanel. As if all this perfection weren't enough, she moved with total self-assurance.

What's your problem, honey? I thought. Split ends?

A few minutes later she spoke to the group,

and I learned that her problem indeed was an end, the end of her husband and two children, who had just been killed in a plane crash. And now this vision of absolute loveliness was afraid to be alone because she was afraid she might kill herself.

Her tragedy reminded me of the ancient wisdom: Never criticize someone until you have walked a mile in his shoes. No matter how good someone's life may look from a distance, she may be living with unseen, unbearable suffering and sorrow.

Joan, I told myself, if that woman can get out of bed in the morning after losing her entire family, you can survive suicide, theatrical failure, and bankruptcy. You've got Melissa, the most important thing of all. So stop feeling sorry for yourself.

And I suddenly remembered an old Russian proverb that my mother used to quote: "If everyone hung their troubles out on the wash line, people would see what others were going through and then take their own troubles back in."

By being with other people in a support group, you can see a hell of a lot of laundry: You can see how many people share your troubles and how many make your troubles look almost like blessings. You can see how wide the range of "normal" behavior is and how many different and valid ways there are to cope with grief.

"Your friends and family may have strong expectations about how you should behave," says psychologist Janis Heil. "And those pressures can be unbearable. Being in a group . . . can give you the strength to resist them."

The truth is, of course, that *all* of us are crazy in one way or another. But whatever your craziness may be — short of thinking you're a dolphin or wanting to make love in Penn Station — it *mustn't* stop you from functioning and moving ahead. If it does, you've got to lie down and tell someone about it — or do the telling standing up.

Don't share just your craziness: Share your victories too, no matter how small they are at first. Giving my self-help lectures is a kind of therapy for me as well. Sharing my battlefield knowledge with a roomful of other survivors helps to keep me going. Of course, I also like getting laughs, from survivors and the world at large. How could I ever complain when I've had such a splendid career? To tell a joke in front of six thousand people, hear them laugh, and get paid for it definitely beats saying, "Is that for here or to go?"

Even after you're feeling better, stay in group therapy awhile because your insights will help others and make you feel strong and capable. Even consider volunteering to work with people who've had a loss like yours.

"Hey, I know how to get through this," you can say. "Let me show you how."

9

MIRROR, MIRROR, ON YOUR WALL

There are people who teach motivation. There are also people who read tea leaves. It seems to me that motivation cannot be learned: It has to come from deep inside you. Sometimes it's dormant and needs a jump start from you; and sometimes it's alive from your first moment in the delivery room.

Consider this memorable example. There was once a nineteen-year-old girl from Brooklyn named Barbara Streisand — she had the extra *a* in those days — who wanted to be a Broadway singing star. Looking around at the new shows that were casting, she noticed one called *The Sound of Music* and decided that it would be acceptable for launching her. This dark-haired, dark-eyed girl with a face that said Young Hadassah wanted to play an Austrian Catholic. It would have made more sense for me to want to play Scarlett O'Hara.

And so Barbara Streisand auditioned to be one of the von Trapp children in *The Sound of Music*, but she was turned down because the producers didn't think that one of the von Trapp children should look as though she kept a kosher home. However, Barbara Streisand sang so well that an assistant producer at *The Sound of Music* sent her to audition for another new show, one called *I Can Get It for You Wholesale*. She got the part of a minor character called Miss Marmelstein, made audiences forget every other character onstage, and has been working pretty steadily ever since.

Yes, even with the world's best therapist, you will survive and go on to re-create your life only if you have the motivation, the inner drive, to do so. There is truth to the old joke: "How many therapists does it take to change a light bulb?" "One, but the light bulb really has to *want* to change."

After Edgar killed himself, I was tempted to stay mired in memories and regrets. In fact, I thought more than once about becoming our family's second suicide; but I knew that I couldn't leave Melissa alone; I had to show her that there were responses to tragedy other than the one her father had chosen.

In those first awful days after the suicide, I wanted to get into bed and take up permanent residence there. But I kept telling myself again and again: You have to be strong for Melissa. You have to get through this for her. This responsibility to Melissa turned out to be my salvation: It was the only thing that could have gotten me out of bed and made me feel the need to go on.

Moreover, I realized that my daughter wasn't the only one depending on me: Several employees counted on me for their livelihood and a couple of dogs needed me, too. Spike had been my constant companion for years, giving me the unconditional love that can only come from a pet — maybe not a goldfish, but certainly a dog. For this reason therapists tell us to look to every living thing for the reason to go on.

"I was in such shock and pain after my husband was killed in a plane crash," says Debra, "that I didn't get out of bed for almost a month. My mom had come to help with the kids, who were nine and eleven. Well, one day Mom came into my room and said, 'Debra, you may be thirty-nine years old, but I'm still your mother and can still tell you a thing or two. Your girls need a mother *now*, and if you don't get out of bed and start being that mother again, they're going to have serious problems.' It was the jolt I needed, a reminder of the people who needed me."

People who need people, as Barbra Streisand used to sing, *are* the luckiest people in the world. Knowing that someone is counting on you means you simply aren't allowed to leave the arena of active life, where Teddy Roosevelt felt that all of us belong.

When the gorgeous beauty salon of my friend Kenneth Battelle burned down eight years ago, he knew that he somehow had to keep going for the more than ninety employees who were counting on him. Because Kenneth had lost not just his business but also all his art, antiques, and mementos, he could have gone into a permanent funk, but he didn't have the luxury to do so: His staff had grown sentimental about getting their checks. When I called him the day after the fire and invited him to come for tea and sympathy, he said, "Sorry. I have to meet a broker to check out a new space."

It would probably be another day or two before he could give me a comb-out.

Who is counting on *you* — besides the IRS? Make a list of the people; and then, if you're tempted to go suck your thumb in a corner, suck in your stomach instead and keep moving on.

You say you can't think of a single person who needs you to get out of bed? Then sign up for some regular volunteer work. Read to children in a hospital. Deliver meals to people who can't leave home.

When I moved to New York, I began volunteering for God's Love We Deliver, a

138

group that gives meals to homebound AIDS patients. The first time the staff saw me come in, they must have thought: Celebrity! Get her name on the dance invitations! Tell her that all she needs to do is lend her name!

But I didn't want to be window dressing: I wanted to *wash* windows if I had to. I wanted to donate my time, to take food to someone who needed company. I wanted to give a laugh to someone who could really use one. Hell, *I* could really have used one, but I couldn't worry about myself right now. I just knew that someone was counting on me to get out of bed and get dressed. After convincing the God's Love people to let me take suppers to AIDS patients, I forgot all about my own misery and dropped my new hobby of feeling sorry for myself.

In short, get off your back and give something back — and then watch the happy ricochet. You'll pardon the sermon; I really don't mean to sound like the Reverend Rivers. I am certainly not a puritan (how hard I once tried to be a tramp!); but I confess that the American mania for total retirement bothers me because doing nothing all day is, in the words of Cole Porter, "my idea of nothing to do." Whether you've just been through a tragedy or merely the Lincoln Tunnel, the way to save yourself, the way to make both your mind and body strong, is to look outside yourself.

"Retire?" said Bob Hope at ninety-three. "To *what?*"

At ninety, King Gustav VI of Sweden was still playing tennis. Of course, he didn't go to net much.

And there's another way that you should look outside yourself, whether you're rebounding or at any other time: Look away from your chronological age, because it's not your *real* age; at least it doesn't *have* to be. All of us know people who were middle-aged in their twenties and others who are youthful at sixty-five. You don't have to be a Democrat to appreciate something Bill Clinton once said: "I feel as though I'm sixteen. I have always felt sixteen. Hillary, on the other hand, has always been forty-five."

In a sitcom of the seventies called *Fish*, Abe Vigoda made the same point.

"I was young once," he said. "I was no good at it."

Well, there's no reason why *you* can't be good at it for ninety years, never counting your candles and motivated all the way.

10

THE ROLE OF
YOUR LIFE

If none of these methods has triggered your motivation, if the help of a therapist, the support of friends, or the plight of others hasn't lifted you out of your funk, there's one other way: Look for role models you can emulate. Look at the lives of strong men and women who have shown that the human spirit is indomitable.

I had to do such looking myself. Even knowing that Melissa was counting on me, and even knowing the rewards of making visits for God's Love We Deliver, I still had days when I felt like going to bed for a couple of years.

"I can't do it, I just can't do it," I said again and again.

But Helen Keller and Frieda Warburg Rosenberg and a few other women wouldn't let me give up. Whenever I'm tempted to give up, I think of these women who have gotten through the toughest of times; and I tell myself: If they could triumph, so could I. A bit of poetic license for my ego, of course, to put myself in the same class as Helen Keller; I probably should have used someone I more closely resembled: Helen of Troy.

Frieda Warburg Rosenberg would have

been delighted for me to use her; she was Edgar's mother. Born in Germany, she and her husband, a prominent film producer, lived in comfort until the early 1930s. When Hitler took power, she and her husband quickly moved to Denmark, a much more hospitable place for Jews. Frieda, then in her mid-thirties, learned a new language and created a new home for her husband and son.

And then one day she saw a swastika painted on the side of her house, and she knew it was time to move again. She took the family to Cape Town, South Africa, where again she had to learn a new language; and to earn a living, she and her husband became undertakers. A few years later Frieda decided that America would have better opportunities for Edgar, so she went to New York. She had sold her few Cape Town belongings to finance the family's new start in the United States. As she had done in Germany and Denmark, she left everything else behind.

For the third time in ten years, Frieda started a new life. For the third time, now in her mid-forties, she started with nothing, made a home for her family, and never complained.

I told myself: If Frieda could survive when things were really rotten, so could I. There were no mother-in-law jokes in my family.

My second role model was my own mother, Beatrice Molinsky. Born in St. Petersburg, Russia, in 1906, she grew up in an extremely wealthy home. When the revolution came in 1917, my grandmother fled with the children and any money that was left. Suddenly, instead of sleeping in a bed in a mansion, my mother slept on two hard chairs pushed together, in a cold-water flat.

But she never complained. To put herself through school, she worked double shifts in a blouse factory. She graduated with honors. When she married my father and he was starting his own medical practice, she spent hours at subway stations, giving out handbills with his office number and fees. And, after a full day of subway advertising, she came home to do all the cooking and cleaning. My dad, who became a very successful doctor, often talked about the guts and strength of his blushing bride.

Today my roster of role models includes not only these two marvelous women but also such contemporaries as Jean Harris, the school headmistress who was convicted of killing her lover, the doctor who had devised the Scarsdale Diet. According to Harris, the killing had been accidental; but no matter *what* the killing had been, she was poorly represented in court. Instead of being acquitted or given a minor sentence, she was given a long one. It was outrageously unjust.

Harris could have spent her time in prison sulking in bitter resentment, but she had too much class, too much gumption, to be unproductive. She organized a school for less educated inmates and also a nursery for the children of her fellow convicts. Moreover, after her release, she continued to do volunteer work at the prison. Could there be a better example of how noble the human spirit can be?

Yes, one of my role models is an ex-con. In fact, so are two others: Nelson Mandela and Mahatma Gandhi. But my mother-in-law was clean.

When the youngest son of my friends Steve Lawrence and Eydie Gorme died suddenly a few years ago, I wondered how they would be able to survive. The death of a child is life's cruelest blow. But Steve and Eydie *did* survive. They missed their son desperately, of course; but they used their love for each other, for their friends, and for their work to let them keep moving forward. And if Steve and Eydie can keep moving forward, I have often told myself, then so can I.

Does all this sound like a half-time talk in the locker room at Notre Dame? I guess it does. But why do you think that Notre Dame is always the way to bet?

You laugh at college football fans sticking their fingers in the air to tell the world they're number one. And sometimes you'd like to respond with a different finger of your own. But Vince Lombardi was right: Winning *is* the only thing. However, he had the opponent wrong: It's not eleven steroid-soaked men, it's the adversity of life.

Also on my list is a woman from Puerto Rico named Sally Jessy Raphael.

"I was fired eighteen times," Sally says. "And every time I was more determined than ever to be successful. When I was coming up through the ranks, women were not even *on* the air; they had no presence in radio or TV. So I was competing with the enemy — men — the very ones who were firing me. But through all the firings, I always felt that I was right and they were wrong. I took that rejection and turned it into *direction.* Have I gotten used to rejection? Absolutely not. But I have learned how to endure."

High on the role model list, too, is Bob Hope. No entertainer in American history has ever achieved more: Bob is the *only* one who was ever supremely successful in every medium: vaudeville, radio, movies, and TV. You probably think it was all a walk in the park for Bob. Wrong: In his early days, Bob considered *sleeping* in the park:

"One day in 1928 I was standing in front of the Woods Theatre Building in Chicago. I'd been getting ten dollars a show, but now I couldn't get even that. Nobody knew me. My name was Leslie Hope, so I decided to change it to Bob Hope because it sounded more chummy; but I was still starving. I couldn't get a date, I wasn't eating well, and my laundry was piling up. I was just about ready to go home to Cleveland to get a full meal and my laundry done when a friend of mine walked up. He was a very successful vaudevillian named Charlie Coolly.

" 'How you doing?' he said.

"I could have kept my pride and said I was doing great, but instead I told the truth: 'I'm starving,' I replied.

" 'Come with me.'

"So he introduced me to his booker, who said, 'I can give you one day at the West Inglewood Theatre. Will twenty-five dollars be all right?'

"And that was the date that got me rolling."

So who are the role models on your list? Almost every successful person had to overcome at least one major obstacle. Look at Wilma Rudolph, the Olympic sprint champion. Would you believe that she had childhood polio?

Look at Christopher Reeve, who reminds us that sometimes obstacles appear at the peak of success. In 1995 an accident made him a paraplegic. The following year he narrated an HBO documentary about physical handicaps, directed an HBO drama, and performed in a CBS film. If Christopher Reeve can be cheerful, optimistic, and productive, then let me hear no moaning from you — unless it's during good sex, of course.

11

ON LIFE'S TRAMPOLINE

There's one role model I forgot to mention, and he may be the best of the twentieth century. He is certainly the century's comeback kid: Winston Churchill. One of his biographers, William Manchester, summed up Churchill's life with this phrase: "He does not know how to give in." Churchill himself put it even more ringingly when he said, "Never, never, never give up!"

There were many times in his thrilling life when giving up seemed to be the only choice he had.

One day in 1932, when Churchill was out of office and seemingly lost in the political wilderness, Nancy, Lady Astor, who gave new meaning to the word "bitch," was having an audience with Josef Stalin in the Kremlin.

"And what about Churchill?" Stalin asked her. "What is he doing these days?"

"Oh, Churchill!" Lady Astor replied. "He's finished!"

Eight years later, at the age of sixty-six, Churchill began his role in the saving of Western civilization.

Perhaps Lady Astor took such glee in pronouncing Churchill dead because of an exchange they'd once had at a London dinner party.

"Winston," she said to him, "if I were your wife, I would put poison in your soup."

"And if I were your husband," he replied, "I'd drink it."

Yes, if you're having trouble getting yourself to move ahead, role models can be fine inspirations. However, perhaps the best inspiration of all is a somewhat less noble one: the sweet taste of revenge.

In 1952, in the promotion department of *Esquire* magazine, there was a young man who went on to produce a lifetime of such sweets for himself. He asked for a fifteen-dollar-a-week raise and was turned down. Hugh Hefner then left *Esquire*; founded his own magazine, called *Playboy*, and dealt *Esquire* a blow from which it never really recovered.

And here's another delicious one. There was once a student at Harvard who wanted to conduct the school band. The young man was already a brilliant musician, but, for some unfathomable reason, his bid to conduct the Harvard band was rejected. And so Leonard Bernstein went on to conduct other things, like the greatest orchestras of the world.

"That rejection became part of my motivation in the outside world," he said. "I kept saying: *I'll show them!*"

This hunger to avenge past put-downs can keep you going when traditional drive goes into neutral for you. The "I'll show them!" urge is certainly a big element in what makes me get up in the morning, particularly when I'm up against the toughest times. My comeback was fundamentally inspired by a desire to show the network executives, the critics, and the tabloids that they couldn't get rid of me so easily. Don't you think that revenge was the sweetest snack when I became Barry Diller's biggest star at QVC a few years after he had fired me at Fox?

And it was a sultan's feast for a couple of actors who'd been treated badly when they worked as lowly contract players at RKO. After leaving the studio, they both went into TV, did quite well, and then Lucille Ball and Desi Arnaz *bought* RKO.

When I was starting out, there was a chiseling little agent, Jeff Funk, who used to book me for performances in the Catskills.

"I'll book you at five dollars a night and take fifty cents' commission," he told me.

Years later I learned that he'd been charging *fifty dollars a night* for my act. Not only had he been lying to me, but he'd been cheating a starving kid out of forty-five dollars a night.

Fifteen years later I was the star of the show at Caesar's Palace in Las Vegas, and I got a call from Jeff: He was in the casino with his wife and he'd like to see my show — if only it weren't so expensive.

"That bastard!" said Edgar. "The nerve of him! I hope you're not planning to pick up the check."

"Of course," I replied, "and I'm going to relish every second of it."

Not only did I pick up the check, but I invited Jeff and his wife to my dressing room. And I thought: Well, just look at what's happened. Jeff is still stuck in his little office, making shady deals for struggling comics, and my name is a household word.

At that moment I may have felt more hubris than the gods like you to show. After all, another household word is Drāno.

But I had showed Jeff; and several years later I vowed to show all those who had turned their backs on me in Hollywood; and then, a decade later, I vowed to show all those who had swindled me out of my business in New York.

Fox canceled me? Well, I swore, I'll get another show *and* I'll win an Emmy too! Regal Communications crushed me with thirty-seven million dollars of debt? Well, I'll build an even bigger company and let Regal's CEO drown in jealousy.

With "I'll show them!" as my mantra, I started fighting my way back.

After *Sally Marr* closed, I went to hear Barbra Streisand at New York's Paramount. I had known Barbra when we both were starting out, when she was still Barbara with the traditional *a* and I was Joan Molinsky. I had hoped that the concert would give me a lift, but it turned into just another blow to my self-esteem. Barbra was delighting a theater full of adoring fans, and I was out of work. The contrast between our careers — at that moment mine was invisible — only heightened my pain.

During intermission I met an old friend, a man who said, "Joan, I was just telling my wife about your play closing after those great reviews. We decided that you have the worst luck of anybody we've ever met."

He wasn't trying to be unkind, but his words stung. Losing my play was bad enough, but being pitied was even worse. At that moment I began to burn with rage and with the desire to stop stewing and start doing.

The next morning, I began making calls to set up meetings. And all the while I kept thinking: Just watch me, mister. I'll show you the kind of luck you've never seen! Luck to come back again and again.

With those calls I was making my *own* luck. I was taking the first steps toward my comeback, for I knew that fantasies of revenge shouldn't merely *be* fantasies: They should be turned into your spur to action and success.

And I've talked to so many other survivors who've taken the same happy road back.

"After the hurricane had hit my house," says Karen, "I knew my ex-husband was thinking: Karen will never get through this. He'd always put me down and thought I couldn't survive on my own. Well, now I was determined to prove to him — and myself — what a competent woman I was. I would deal with the insurance people and then do everything necessary to rebuild my life. What kept me going was the mental picture of my ex-husband coming to the door of a great new home to pick up the boys for the weekend and being *knocked out* by what I had done!"

Another guest at one of my lectures used this same excellent incentive.

"I was fired because a young hotshot had taken over my department at the public relations agency and gotten rid of everyone over forty," says Len, who was fifty-four when he was fired. "I had grounds to sue for age discrimination, but the case would've taken years, and I had two hefty college tuition bills. So I said to myself: You want to see what an old man is made of? I'll show you. And I opened my own small agency. Within months, many of my old firm's clients left to work with me. Can you imagine the pleasure I got when I called the new boss to tell him to send me different files for accounts that would now be paying *me?!* I was just sorry I couldn't see the jerk's face."

The triumphs of people like Karen and Len prove again that no adversity can stop someone who has enough motivation. Let yourself be like Winston Churchill, returning from obscurity to save the Western world *and* give Lady Astor a kick in the ass. Simply do not know the meaning of the word "quit." But certainly be ready to use a few other four-letter words.

12

WITH A LAUGH FOR YOUR HEART

Although motivation is the best response to adversity, laughter is a great response, too. This doesn't mean that you should give a drowning man a laugh instead of a rope. It means . . . well, if you don't know, you're in more trouble than you think. Scientists, however, *have* recently learned a remarkable fact: When you put your facial muscles into a smile for just ten seconds, natural juices in your system start flowing and trick you into being happy — whether or not the smile is heartfelt. It's better to be a fake at happiness than an honest depressive.

Not only is laughter wonderful for your morale, but it's actually good for your physical well-being. A hundred laughs a day are the equivalent of ten minutes of aerobic exercise: Researchers at Stanford University have found that laughter improves respiration, muscular function, blood pressure, and heart rate, and can even relieve pain. In fact, hearty laughter raises the heart rate to more than 120 beats a minute, as hard as your heart pumps during sex — and laughing doesn't mess up your hair. If a couple routinely laughed during sex, they would live forever.

A few years ago, the noted editor of the

Saturday Review, Norman Cousins, became the victim of a strange neurological malady that doctors didn't know how to treat. While they groped for a cure, Cousins tried an experiment: He would see if he could laugh his way to health. Because he had always felt that *Candid Camera* was the funniest TV show, he took dozens of tapes of *Candid Camera* to a hotel room, got into bed, and spent a couple of weeks laughing. The improvement in his health was so dramatic that his case made the medical journals.

In other words, a doctor could say to someone who wasn't feeling well, "Take two monologues and call me in the morning."

Instinctively I have always turned to humor to help me heal; and not long after Edgar's suicide, I turned to it again. I took Melissa back to her room in a house near the campus of the University of Pennsylvania in West Philadelphia. It was a typical off-campus student house: chipped paint, rotten beams, scattered dirty clothing, and a floor sticky with beer. You would have had to fix up the place a bit before it could be condemned.

When we walked in, Melissa's friends were uncomfortable. No one had seen her since Edgar's death, and they were unsure of how to react. There was an awkward silence, and then I said: "Melissa, thank God your father's dead. If he saw you living here, he'd kill himself all over again."

It was a variation of the line I had used to get a smile from Melissa when we'd had that tense dinner in a restaurant shortly after Edgar's suicide, but again it worked and broke the tension. In this Philadelphia branch of Tobacco Row, Missy's friends saw that she and I were laughing, and then laughed with us. And the laughter bound us together.

Unfortunately, student rooms were the only rooms I could play in those first painful months after Edgar's death. The week after the funeral, my agent came to the house to see me. I thought he was there for a condolence call, and in a way he was. What had died was my career. Instead of giving me a basket of fruit, he decided that *I* was now the lemon, and he gave me back my agency contract.

"Joan, I hate to say this," he said without seeming to hate it all that much, "but no one will want to book a comedienne whose husband has just killed himself; it would make audiences too uncomfortable."

My agent's brush-off would have been a perfect excuse for me to quit comedy, but

I've never wanted to play the role of victim. Too many people are playing it already, and I can't stand being part of a mob. Moreover, I desperately needed to keep working, rather than sit home and feel sorry for myself. I needed the charge an audience always gave me, an audience bigger than Melissa's roommates. I also needed a few laughs myself.

And so I told Dorothy Melvin to start making calls.

"Book me somewhere," I told her. "Anywhere."

I was ready to play the lounge at Penn Station.

Dorothy didn't book me there, of course: She found the only place that wanted me: a tiny comedy club outside Buffalo that held eighty-four people *if* they all came. I remembered the words of Judy Holliday: "Oh well, it's only humiliation."

However, another role model of mine, Eleanor Roosevelt, once said that you cannot be humiliated unless you *let* yourself be. Do you think she might have made an exception for someone who had gone from her own network television show to a north-country coat room?

As I stood backstage at that comedy club, wondering if the act after me would be a koala playing a kazoo, I told myself: Well,

Joan, this may be just a little better than talking to yourself, but at least you're doing what you know and love.

Suddenly I was up onstage, overwhelmed by a fear that they wouldn't laugh, a fear that I might not have it anymore. Boldly I decided to cut the tension about Edgar by discussing him right at the start.

"As you certainly know," I said, "it's been a lousy year for me. My husband killed himself. He asked me to have his ashes spread at Neiman Marcus because he knew that way I'd come to visit him every day."

For a moment I heard only a massive gasp. And then I heard the laughter that had always been my basic reason for getting up in the morning. The audience was happy to feel at ease, and I was even happier to know that I still had the gift I cherish most.

When you're going through a tough time, your friends may feel uncomfortable about doing any laughing; they may opt for steady solemnity. Well, let them know that you're solemnly in favor of laughter, which dispels tension and creates outlets for feelings that confuse and overwhelm us. The minute the space shuttle blew up, there was a joke about it; there *had* to be. And not long after a plane crashed in the Everglades, I read this one on the Internet: "ONE ALLIGATOR TO AN-

OTHER: Not bad for airline food."

And moments after the O. J. Simpson verdict, my phone rang with this one: "Good news: They've found Hitler. Bad news: He's being tried in Los Angeles."

Whenever I'm in terrible pain, I particularly enjoy black humor. So do many other people, and this is nothing new. Right after Lincoln's assassination, this line was going around: "But except for that, Mrs. Lincoln, how did you like the play?"

Many of my friends share my flair for black humor. A few years ago one of them lost his house in the Los Angeles fires. When a reporter asked him how he felt about the devastation, my friend replied: "Well, I'm finally caught up on my paperwork."

There is absolutely no better way to relieve tension than laughter. At one point in my seminars, usually after a truly heart-wrenching moment, I say to the audience, "Now everyone turn around and look at the person next to you and say, 'I'm so glad.' " And all of them think: "How nice. Joan wants us to connect to each other in sympathy." And then I add, "I'm not you." It breaks the tension and everyone is able to go on.

Bring humor into your life in any way you can; I simply can't overstate its value. Could there be any medicine more healing than thinking of Victor Borge meeting a friend and asking him: "Was it you or your brother who died?" Or thinking of my favorite line of artistic criticism: "Wagner's music isn't as bad as it sounds." Or Oscar Wilde's sublime line: "I was married once. It was the result of a misunderstanding between myself and a young woman."

You get the point: There is no narcotic like humor, as in the story by Robert Benchley that begins, "Around 1845 or a quarter to nine . . ."

"After Karl got his HIV test back," says a man named Bill, "we both sat in bed all weekend and cried. After a while I went to the video store for us. I was about to check out *Terms of Endearment* when my eye fell on *Monty Python and the Holy Grail*. I hadn't seen it in years, so I picked it up too. When Karl and I watched that movie, we laughed until the couch shook. And we felt wonderful."

I'm always hunting for things that will make me laugh. After *Sally Marr* had closed and my business was a shambles, I spent two days in my apartment with the lights dimmed and the curtains drawn, enjoying a good dose of misery. But after a while I remembered what a tonic humor had been after Edgar's death; and so, I decided to retrace my steps of recovery to help me through this second round of losses. I went back to reading Robert Benchley and I looked at my favorite *New Yorker* cartoons.

And after Benchley and the cartoons, I finished my great mood reversal by just playing mental tapes of favorite theatrical lines, such as this one from *A Funny Thing Happened on the Way to the Forum*: "ONE ROMAN *(to another, while examining a bottle of wine)*: Was one a good year?"

The other mental tape I like to play is the one that says, as I keep meeting new people, "I like these people. I'm going to have a good time today." I'm not saying that you should play that tape at a tax audit or gum surgery, but the prophecy often does become a self-fulfilling one. I not only like to make people laugh professionally, I also like to make them smile offstage. Every day when I take a long walk through my Manhattan neighborhood, I enjoy making several doormen smile. There have been times when I've thought that someday I'll be playing only to doormen, but if it ever comes to that for me, I won't do twenty-seven of them single file: I'll collect them all in one building and work the lobby.

13

THE BEST FOUR-LETTER WORD IS HOPE

Another way to generate your own happiness is to be generous with praise. Whenever I like something about a person, whether it's a new haircut or an old vase, I always pay him or her a compliment. And, on the flip side, never point out anything that might make someone feel uncomfortable. Besides never saying such words as "Didn't they have a toupée to match your sideburns?" or "Do you think that style will ever come back?" also be thoughtful about the little things. It's not necessary to tell a friend at a party about a rip in her pantyhose, unless you're carrying a spare.

Do everything you can to make people feel comfortable. When having dinner with friends, I always make eye contact with everyone at the table. I strive to be like the hostess in the following story, which may be apocryphal, but who cares?

There was once an elegant dinner party at which the hostess suddenly noticed that one of the less sophisticated guests was starting to drink from the finger bowl. The hostess then lifted her own finger bowl and started to drink so that the guest with the misplaced thirst would not be embarrassed.

"When you're an upbeat person," says a

woman named Faye, "other upbeat people want to be around you. That's why I put a positive spin on everything. I even sent out a colorful divorce announcement."

The problem with pessimism is that it's too easy; it's like betting on the sun to rise in the East. Of *course* you're going to lose more often than you win; of *course* more things will turn out wrong than right; but is it any fun living that way? Or any adventure? And remember what Helen Keller said about adventure: It's the essence of life.

Many experts feel that you can learn to look up rather than down. In his popular book *Learned Optimism*, psychologist Martin E. Seligman says: "A pessimistic attitude may seem so deeply rooted as to be permanent. I have found, however, that pessimists can in fact learn to be optimists."

Optimism allows you to keep life's small aggravations, frustrations, and setbacks in proportion. It reminds you of that wonderful two-line philosophy:

1. Don't be bugged by the small stuff.
2. It's *all* small stuff.

Okay, it's not Socrates or even Regis Philbin, but it's pretty damn wise. And I do try to live this philosophy, as I did one cold winter night with friends in Paris. Eager to celebrate our last night together in style, we had made reservations at a very chic restaurant and then hopped into a cab. The driver was a member in good standing of the I-Hate-Stupid-Tourists Club, who decided to enrich international ill will by playing a little trick on us and dropping us even farther from the restaurant then we'd been at the start. There wasn't another cab in sight. It was late, it was cold, and everyone was hungry. The evening had the potential to be memorably awful.

Suddenly, however, we saw a little café and one of us said, "Hey, let's eat there."

We all went into the tiny, family-run café and had an absolutely marvelous dinner. There wasn't another tourist in sight; and, because the menus were in French, we had to order in French, and we felt as though we were having a real evening in Paris. For all I knew I was ordering the local version of a Whopper, but I didn't care because this little adventure was so much fun.

We could have said: "We have reservations at the other place. *Damn* that driver. *Damn* Paris." But, as *Casablanca*'s Rick knew when he was there with Elsa, Paris wasn't for damning. Because a cab driver had possessed the navigational flair of Columbus, and because of the way we had rolled with his directional dumbness, I had a wonderful dinner that transformed that evening into my favorite memory of the entire trip.

We had improvised. And if you don't think that *all* life is improvisation, then you haven't been paying attention. Life is what happens to you while you're making other plans.

Happiness comes from a willingness to make the best of a bad situation, to seize the moment and live it as cheerfully as you can. Is that a cliché? Of course. How do you think clichés become clichés? Because they're so damn true.

I'm not going to tell you that life is a bowl of cherries. How *could* I when I've gone into a different bowl so many times? But precisely *because* I've lost so much, I make it a point to savor every good moment I can grab; and I try like hell to maintain a childlike enthusiasm for things, even when the child is saggy and sixty.

Last year a friend of mine named Benjamin was going through a painful divorce and wanted to talk to me.

"Let's have lunch," I told him.

"Le Cirque or La Grenouille?" he said, naming two Manhattan restaurants that are never confused with a Roy Rogers.

"Neither," I said. "Let me pick it."

And I took him to a Royal Canadian Pancake House, where no royal *anyone* ever ate. Its tables were Formica and its pancakes formidable, literally fourteen inches in diameter! Benjamin always dressed as if he were headed for Buckingham Palace. To see him at the pancake house amid all the sweatshirts and jeans, trying to manipulate those huge pancakes, gave us both a laugh and gave him a blessed break from his routine.

"You know," he said, halfway through his pancakes, "this is the most fun I've had in months."

When the most fun that someone has had in months comes from eating big pancakes, his life has been no Mardi Gras.

I like to have this kind of fun every day and you can too if you try to look at life as an adventure and avoid settling into a routine. Change more than your underwear every morning: Change your routine. When I have an errand to run, I never plan what street I should take. One going in the right direction, of course — I'm not that French cabbie — but never the same day after day. By taking a different route, who knows whom I'll meet?

Maybe I'll run into a business acquaintance who has a great idea, or maybe I'll run into an old boyfriend and wonder what my life would have been like as Mrs. Seymour Ravachevsky, the wife of Scarsdale's best podiatrist.

In spite of all my "bad" luck, I truly appreciate how really lucky I've been. If there's one thing that drives me crazy, it's someone who takes a comfortable life for granted. Having a bad hair day, honey? Well, pick up the newspaper and look at all the people who are having a bad staying alive day. Robert Louis Stevenson summed it up when he wrote:

The world is so full of a number of things,
I'm sure we should all be as happy as kings.

He must have meant Alan King, the comedian, and his wife; these days the other kind are considerably less merry.

The point is to appreciate all the goodies that are out there, and to vary your tasting of them. A routine is what I do on the stage; I try to keep that word from ever applying to the rest of my life.

Nature, in fact, doesn't really *want* you to have a routine. Fats Waller took a place in the pantheon of philosophers simply by reminding us, "One never knows, do one?"

"It's so easy to get into a rut," says a woman named June, "particularly when you're going through a tough time. When I was going through the pain of infertility, I kept going back to my old gym and taking the same aerobics class at the same time, never varying my routine. One day — just for a lift — I did something different and signed up for an adult beginners' ballet class at the local Y. Well, I had so much fun! The dancing was really challenging. I put on little pink slippers and pretended I was a ballerina; it took me outside my shell for an hour twice a week. And then I bought myself a bike, which I hadn't ridden since the seventh grade. It was incredibly liberating to ride around different neighborhoods."

To shake the cobwebs from your mind, you might even try changing your whole lifestyle by doing something dramatic and swapping lives with someone else for a while. I don't mean Marla Trump, but maybe your sister in the suburbs. Offer your sister and her husband the use of your apartment in the city while you take over their lawn and their kids. A weekend with their kids might make you think harder about birth control, but the change will still be worthwhile.

If you don't feel brave enough to swap lifestyles, try trading clothing for a little while. Are you bored with the same old outfits? Then find a friend who's the same size and change a few clothes with her; for no expense you might get a lift. Or see if RuPaul has something that might look good on you.

Even something as simple as reading aloud to a child can give you a fresh perspective and a wonderful lift. There has never been a lovelier book than *Goodnight, Moon.* And maybe you've forgotten how it turns out. Are you tired of the daily smorgasbord of horror in the newspapers? Then read *Frog and Toad* to a small friend. Read the story in which Frog tells Toad that he can't do anything today because he wrote his whole day's schedule on a list and then lost the list — and one of the activities on the schedule *wasn't* losing the list. Well, that happens to be the very point I've been making in a nonamphibian way. As Toad tells Frog, you've just got to wing it.

From time to time it's also wise to readjust your biological clock. If you're a night person, take a look at the dawn — from the other side, that is; start there for a few days and see how wondrous mornings can be. From 6 to 9 A.M., before the day has a chance to head down the drain, the world is intoxicatingly fresh. "Oh What a Beautiful Morning" can apply to Rhode Island as well as Oklahoma.

One day when I was feeling down, I made

myself go up: to the open top of a double-decker tour bus, where I spent the next two hours looking at New York, my hometown, with a tourist's eyes. And being on that bus and looking down at this masterpiece reminded me of what a certain young lady in a musical sings: "What good is sitting alone in your room? Life is a cabaret."

Yes, of course the cabaret has some bad acts, but you'll never know that by surfing channels in a dark room. Just watch E! and QVC for two or three hours, and then go out and surf the world.

14

A WORLD FOR HEALING

If you want to move forward after loss and depression, you have to create a healing environment. Does that sound like a suggestion to build a hospital? Well, I apologize for any phrase in this book that accidentally resembles psychobabble. By "healing environment" I simply mean a place where you feel contented, a place you look forward to entering every time you open the front door.

After Edgar's suicide I quickly realized that my house in Beverly Hills was no longer a place to heal my wounds and plan a new life. Edgar and I had lived there for fourteen years. In that house, we had raised Melissa, thrown birthday and anniversary parties, had Thanksgiving and Passover dinners and sleepovers for Girl Scouts. In spite of these golden memories, I was now a woman alone, and the house was suddenly too big and empty and filled with memories of a life that no longer existed.

I began spending a lot of time in New York City. I had grown up in suburban Larchmont and spent my early years as a comic in Greenwich Village. Unlike my painful recent past in Los Angeles, my New York history was an ancient happy one. In New York, I had friends not in show business, friends who wouldn't remind me of everything I'd just lost.

Although Melissa didn't want me to sell our California house, my friend Tommy Corcoran began taking me to see apartments for sale in New York. And one afternoon, on a lark, he took me to see an apartment in what once had been the mansion of J. P. Morgan's daughter. It looked more like the home of Morgan the Pirate: rotting walls, broken windows, warped floors, and rubble in every direction. It made Melissa's apartment at Penn look like the Taj Mahal.

When Tommy took one look at the place, he started to laugh; and while he was laughing, I said, "I'll take it."

Remember what I told you about the value of changing your life? Of course, that doesn't mean that you should move to a toxic waste site.

This old Morgan place wasn't toxic, but early waste was its period. To show you what a dump I had given my heart to, the real estate agent tried to talk me out of it. But where he saw a salute to trash, I saw a challenge, something to keep me excited and busy in a period when I had too much time on my hands and too little to be excited about.

The renovation took two years, and I enjoyed every minute of it: I was building a new home where I could feel secure after so much had been taken away from me. I even made a girlish peach-colored bedroom that I had wanted for thirty years, and I picked out curtains and swags and furniture that I — and maybe *only* I — loved but I didn't care. Okay, so *House & Garden* wouldn't do a layout. Okay, so maybe *Modern Recycling* would stop by. This place just happened to be saving my life.

There was a melancholy side, of course: This lifesaving new duplex off Central Park did leave me with mixed feelings. Edgar would never walk through the door; and Melissa would visit often, but she was a college senior now and would never call the apartment home.

"Joan," I said to the freshly gilded moldings on the day I moved in, "this is where you're going to live your new life."

After your own loss, you may not be able to move or renovate, but you can make *some* change in your surroundings, even if you just rearrange the furniture or get a new comforter cover or paint your kitchen. Do you really want the couch that your ex-husband made you buy? The one where he cuddled for hours with the remote control, trying to remote-control you, too?

"As soon as I got rid of all Bob's things," says Meghan, whose husband cleaned out their joint bank account and then withdrew himself from their life, "I used my next paycheck to have my apartment recarpeted. It felt dirty to me because he had lived there. I needed it to look different so I didn't feel rotten every time I walked in."

Kevin, too, found a great release in clearing his home of painful memories.

"For a while after the accident," he says, talking of the injury that left this champion swimmer partly paralyzed, "I kept all my swimming trophies. But they were just a reminder of everything I had lost, so I got rid of them and put different stuff in my room, including a guitar I hadn't played since the seventh grade. I started playing blues again. I didn't like it as much as swimming, but at least it reminded me that there were other things I could do."

I didn't want to keep singing the blues. Last year I looked at the photos on my piano and realized that it was turning into the memorial Steinway: Edgar, my mother, my father, my Aunt Alice, Edgar's parents, Vincent Price and Coral Browne. Although I got rid of none of those bittersweet photos, I did add many new ones to remind myself that life goes on: a picture of Melissa at her college graduation, one of Dorothy on the beach, one of my nephew's adorable children, and one of four friends and me at the Kentucky Derby in colorful hats. Now, instead of depressing me, that piano is a tableau of my life, good times and bad.

As you move around photos and mementos after a loss, you'll have to decide: Does a picture of a vanished friend bring you down or remind you of happy times? And that seashell you picked up when you rented the beach house with friends that summer after college: Does it bring back happy memories or make you think your life will never again be as good as it was when you were twenty-two?

Anything that makes you unhappy — a picture, a memento, a husband — should go out or be hidden away.

When you're grieving, giving things to friends can be comforting. Before selling the house in Beverly Hills, I invited some of Edgar's close friends to take things they wanted to remember him by. Their choices touched me: One man picked only a book whose hidden meaning he and Edgar had often argued about; another said he wanted one of Edgar's raincoats; and Tom Pileggi, Edgar's closest friend, picked a Timex watch Edgar had bought one morning after noticing that his "real" watch was running slow.

Giving some of Edgar's possessions to people who loved him spared me the burden of making my home the Heavenly Gates of Rosenberg. Of course, I still wanted his presence: Seeing his robe still hanging on the bathroom door gave me comfort; and now, almost ten years later, I still keep two of his tweed jackets hanging in my closet. Whittling his wardrobe down to a few things that mean a great deal to me is a metaphor for the way I've moved on: I'll always keep a place in my heart for Edgar; but, just as I've made room in the closet for clothes of my own, I've made room in my life for new friends and new experiences.

To move on with optimism after a death, you need to hold on a bit and to let go a lot. Last year Pete Sampras's beloved coach, Tim Gullikson, died of brain cancer at forty-four. Reeling with grief, Pete lost a few matches to inferior players and wondered if he could ever again be a champion without Tim. He had even left his last Wimbledon trophy on Tim's casket during the services. But then, bit by bit, he found the proper place for Tim in his mind and his heart, got a new coach, and headed for the top again.

Yes, Pete Sampras is still playing every match for Tim Gullikson, just as I hope that

Edgar is hearing every routine of mine (I've had years of experience playing to the dead), but both of us are moving ahead. We're a couple of people who just can't stay stuck in the past.

You absolutely have to use whatever helps to generate your optimism about the future. Why do so many people insist on listening to Billie Holiday and Edith Piaf when they're depressed? Those two women rarely told anyone to have a good day. Tuneful dismay is the last thing you need. If you're feeling down, put on a pretty shirt and/or an upbeat song. It's hard to be blue when you're hearing "New York, New York."

"All those months I was unemployed," says a woman named Bernadette, "I kept wishing I could be far away from Wall Street. I needed an escape but certainly couldn't afford a vacation. So I bought a few samba and reggae tapes and I'd lie on the couch with my eyes closed, picturing myself on a tropical beach. It was certainly more soothing than hearing Bruce Springsteen sing about the unemployed."

Whenever I need a lift, I play show tunes, and you should turn to whatever music makes you feel *better*. No doctor can write a prescription that lifts you like Gershwin; and the baroque boys can put you into an even higher orbit. The famous pianist Oscar Levant was stopped by a cop for speeding and tried to use the intoxicating power of music as an excuse: "I couldn't help it, you just *can't* go slowly when you're listening to Handel."

Music is the greatest sensual gift ever given to humanity; in fact, many intelligent people say it's clearly a better high than sex. And to think: All those years that I was waiting for Mr. Right to call, I could have been "doing it" with Mr. Rossini.

In addition to listening to music whenever you can, cater to your other senses as well. Scientists say that the sense of smell is most closely tied to our memory, so try to fill your home with scents, things like foods and flowers, that remind you of happy times. The scent of citronella always sends me back to happy summers; and a woman who came to one of my lectures used a similar time machine.

"I take one whiff of Coppertone suntan lotion," says Betty, "and suddenly I'm eight years old again, fighting with my kid brother over whose turn it is to use the blue plastic shovel to make sand castles. When you're going through a knockdown divorce, fights over plastic shovels are happy memories."

For me the scent of pine needles has always been a magic carpet ride back to summer camp. Sniffing a pine is heady stuff. I close my eyes, inhale deeply, and I'm back at a lake in Vermont, where I never had to worry about the bill from American Express.

If the smell of baking cookies is a comforting reminder of your own childhood, then bake a batch. If your mother was a lousy cook, then burn a batch. Even scents not linked to memory can improve your mood. Rosemary is said to be soothing, basil calms your nerves, cedar eases anxiety, and patchouli not only relieves depression but is said to be an aphrodisiac too.

I can't guarantee, of course, that patchouli will inspire a guest to devour you on the kitchen floor; but even if he devours only the veal, the mood may be mellower. In whatever way you can, make your whole home a place where everything feels nice: cotton sheets, soft carpets, cloth napkins.

"Sure, Joan," I can hear you saying. "I'll take a second mortgage to get better drapes."

Well, many fine things actually *save* money. For example, cotton sheets last forever, and washable cloth napkins cost less than constantly buying paper ones and are also better for our greater home, planet Earth.

In spite of the fact that randomness seems to govern our lives, I still believe that life is like a movie and you have the power to write your own script. It may not be *Mary Poppins*, but it needn't be *The Bride of Frankenstein*, either. Mine, of course, is *Saint Joan*.

15

GATHER NO MOSS

Needless to say (so why am I saying it?), even the rosiest attitude won't bring you a full, rich life if you're not in action in Teddy Roosevelt's arena, if you do nothing more each day than watch *All My Children* and smile at friends. Sitting on a re-covered sofa and listening to "Put on a Happy Face" will still leave you in neutral. *You* have to get into gear. *You* have to move from surviving to thriving. *You* have to find rewarding ways to occupy your time — or else consider checking into a well-appointed old-age home.

The happiest people I know are the busiest, and every one of them says that the happiness comes from the activity. This feeling is confirmed by sociologist Mihaly Csikszentmihalyi (that must be his stage name), who says that just being busy, whether or not the work succeeds, makes people happy. He says that artists who get lost in their work achieve a satisfaction so rich that it pleases them even more than the finished product.

I hate to say this about one of America's founding geniuses, but Thomas Jefferson made a mistake in the Declaration of Independence. In it he talks about every American's right to the pursuit of happiness; but happiness is not a goal to be pursued: It is a *by-product* of involvement in rewarding activity. People who pursue happiness itself are like greyhounds chasing mechanical rabbits. The truly happy person never has time to wonder if he or she's happy. I love the words of the noted modern psychiatrist, Thomas Szasz: "Happiness is an imaginary condition, formerly often attributed by the living to the dead, now usually attributed by adults to children and by children to adults."

Claiming to offer uninterrupted happiness, the leisure villages have been selling a deadly narcotic to older Americans: Stop any kind of work, drop out of all meaningful activity, leave your home in a real community, and come here to have fun all the time. Well, you *can't* have fun if fun is all you ever have. When every day is Sunday, Sunday doesn't exist.

In luring older Americans to lives of nothing but leisure, these leisure villages are *not* promoting genuine happiness. In its 1995 poll on happiness, *Self* magazine found that the busiest people were the happiest. And when asked what made them happiest at work, 33 percent said challenging projects. Unfortunately one of the challenging projects these days is to keep a job; but people who like challenges always bounce back.

The magazine also asked people how

happy they were when exercising. Fifty-two percent said very happy, 41 percent said somewhat happy, and only 1 percent said not happy at all.

Exercise makes you happy for *two* reasons: The busy-ness factor is one, and the other is the body's endorphins. When you raise your heart rate through vigorous exercise, endorphins flood your system and trigger a euphoria that is better — and more healthful — than any drug.

Moreover, the benefits of exercise linger. In a study of two hundred men and women, psychologists at the University of Illinois found that those who exercised moderately to vigorously were more optimistic than those who were sedentary. It's hard to find a cranky squash player, a gloomy swimmer, or a pessimistic jogger.

A friend of mine is a sixty-three-year-old who plays tennis singles two or three times a week.

"I've never tried cocaine," he tells me, "but it couldn't equal the high that I feel after a match. I absolutely agree with the sign at my court: TENNIS ISN'T A MATTER OF LIFE AND DEATH. IT'S MORE IMPORTANT THAN THAT."

And so, whether life for you right now is a cabaret or a dive, it *is* always a playing field with all kinds of available sports that are guaranteed to lift your spirits and improve your health. There is obviously no way to win against aging. However, regular and vigorous exercise *can* give you a very long tie.

"I was afraid to go back to golf and tennis," says Sheila, "because they'd remind me too much of my husband; we used to play together a lot. So I tried to convince myself that I'd be better off just lounging around the house, sleeping late and taking long walks — a lady of leisure. Well, in two weeks, I was bored out of my head. I signed up for tennis lessons and started playing golf with other women. I was sad to do these things without Allen, but I just couldn't learn to stay in the house."

Learning to stay in the house is a lesson only for toddlers.

After *Sally Marr* closed and my jewelry business went bust, I was in a mood that would've had to lighten a bit to become merely black. Nevertheless, I made sure that all my days were full, even when I was home. I started having meetings to try to set up new projects, no matter how farfetched they seemed. I started making notes for a new screenplay, and I even signed up for a playwriting course. You'd be surprised how many playwrights should take a playwriting course.

I knew that most of my efforts wouldn't lead to a deal signed or a film made. That's the nature of my business: You cast your bread on the waters and often you get back soggy bread. However, the nicer part of the nature of my business is that, whether or not the work ever reaches an audience, you still have had the *pleasure* of doing it. The creation is half the fun; and sometimes it's all the fun you're going to have. It's the only kind of fun Vincent van Gogh ever had. In his entire lifetime he sold just one painting — for fifty francs.

The creative process is a deeply rewarding one. As I wrote a new screenplay and new proposals, I loved seeing the piles of pages grow. Whatever your profession, avocation, or even hobby may be (as long as it's not writing holdup notes), throwing yourself into work can be a wondrous tonic.

"When Karl was diagnosed with AIDS," says Bill, "I promised myself two things: I'd spend as much time with him as possible and I'd keep myself as busy as possible the rest of the time. And I did: I worked harder at the software company than I'd ever done. It was ironic: All this horrible stuff was going on in my life, but I was getting promotions and raises. Work gave me something to focus on instead of the pain to come."

"After I was laid off," says Bernadette, "I sat around the house for seven weeks feeling sorry for myself. I had money saved, but I was really getting depressed. There was a joke going around at the time:

" 'How do you get your broker's attention?'

" 'Oh, waiter!'

"But after laughing, I thought: You know, waitressing isn't such a bad idea. Well, a friend in a restaurant got me a job there. I did a few shifts, just for the heck of it, and then discovered I liked it. And it sure beat spending the day watching shows about alcoholic lesbian nuns and transvestite space aliens."

If you can't work or don't want to, then for God's sake volunteer. No, not for God's sake: for *yours*. There is no better way to get something than to give something back.

"Vanessa was my life," says a woman named Lorreine. "After she was killed, I had nothing to do all day except sit around and cry or wander around the mall, trying to avoid the children's stores. And then I learned about Mothers Against Drunk Driving and I started doing work for them. My

202

work couldn't bring Vanessa back, but it gave me a good way to channel my anger and grief and a productive way to fill my days. Being busy made me feel so much better."

In other words, the silly leisure villages have the message backward: Doing nothing (and endless recreation adds up to nothing) is the worst thing for you. Being productively busy is the best: It can save you from grief, loneliness, and despair. No matter what the cause of your sadness may be, simply rising with a higher purpose than a trip to the john can be a cure. Take some adult education courses, join a gym, start a reading group, collect shrunken heads — any activity that can fill you with enthusiasm and pride.

You simply *must* have a reason to get up in the morning — or at least the early afternoon.

16

BUT KEEP YOUR SEAT BELT FASTENED

ries, and holidays, especially Christmas, are the worst. Even people who've had no loss at all often feel that Christmas is as merry as an Ingmar Bergman movie.

For me the worst pang came at the second Thanksgiving after Edgar's death. Melissa and I decided to celebrate at home, as we had always done, but how would I set the table? For twenty-two years he and I had sat at opposite ends of the Thanksgiving table, and now the thought of putting anyone else at that place just broke my heart.

Be strong, Joan, I told myself; and then I wondered what I was trying to prove. That I was Wonder Woman? Why make myself miserable? I now have Thanksgiving dinner at a round table, which has no head — and livelier conversation too.

Because we miss Edgar most at the holidays, Melissa and I make an effort to build our little family into an extended one at those bittersweet times. For example, after that awful Yom Kippur rejection at Congregation Emanu-El, I swore that Melissa and I would never again enter a temple alone. Every year since, I have bought four tickets and walked in with a group of friends.

And in December I do what I can to blunt the contrast between the holidays now and the ones when Edgar was alive. He and I used to shop in depth and then decorate the house; but the first holiday season after his death, I knew that this pattern would fill me with good old Yuletide despair. Instead of staying in California, Melissa and I flew to New York and checked into a hotel. And then we invited friends to dinner, instead of sitting around wondering what we would have gotten Edgar had he still been alive.

To shake off your own painful memories during the holiday season, try going to a neutral city with a friend, or give a party yourself, or make plans to go somewhere. Do *not* let yourself sit home alone. Home alone was lively for Macaulay Culkin, but it'll be much too quiet for you.

"Christmas is the hardest," says Lorreine. "Every time a toy commercial comes on TV, I wonder what Vanessa would be playing with if she were alive. The smartest thing is not to watch TV between Thanksgiving and New Year's — and to stay out of malls. I do my shopping in August, when it's less painful. My husband and I do celebrate Christmas, but we go on vacation instead of staying in the house. You might call that running away, but it's the only way we get through the holidays."

Yes, the holidays, with their obligatory good cheer, are hard. So is the first time you do anything without the person you've lost — from playing Scrabble to weeding the garden. At these moments people who need people aren't so lucky at all.

"My first birthday without Mitchell was a killer," says a woman named Paula. "I was so used to celebrating with him — at a nice restaurant or a weekend at an inn. The year after we split up, I had no plans for my birthday and I felt terrible. But then I decided I could either feel sorry for myself or give myself a happy birthday. So I threw myself a party: great food, good wine, and a lot of people I was getting friendly with. Of course I felt kind of sad, but I'd also made the day as easy as I could."

If any place or situation is too painful for you to bear, then avoid it. There are still streets in Los Angeles I can't drive down because they make me miss Edgar too much. Time after time I tried to be mature and take those painful memory lanes; and at last I realized it was time for me to take the advice I'd been giving everyone else and be kind to myself. So now Los Angeles is my private maze and I zigzag through it, avoiding the most sensible route and also an ache in my heart.

There are many depressing things, like earthquakes and floods and certain people running for Congress, that you can't avoid knowing about; but for others you *can* be a smart ostrich. When the disease-of-the-week comes on TV and you see that it's the disease afflicting your child, for God's sake change the channel if it's going to upset you.

"Don't stop doing the things you've always enjoyed," says John DeBerry. "Just put a twist on them. Don't stop going to the movies: Just pick a different theater than the one you went to with your ex-husband. Don't stop vacationing in the mountains, but avoid the place you went to with your late wife."

In other words, stop trying to prove how strong you are. Make things as easy as you can for yourself. As Melissa likes to say, "Life's tough. Wear a helmet."

And, of course, accept the fact that no amount of planning will protect you from the random moments of sadness; but you will get through the bad moments and move forward. If *I* can do it, so can you. And bear in mind that, in many instances of loss, there is no complete closure. Don't wait for one: Just move on.

"I know there are going to be times when it's really bad," says Melissa. "When I get married, who's going to walk me down the aisle? Those are the times when I'll just start crying and say, 'I want my father back.' "

"It's been seven years since my mom died," says Mindy, "and I've pretty much gotten used to it. But when something unusual happens, it still hits me hard. I get a promotion at work and I think: I wish I could tell my mom. My husband and I buy a house, and I realize she'll never see it."

And even at smaller moments, an unbearable sadness can sneak up on you.

"A few months after Daddy died," Melissa says, "I had parked my car in front of a thrift shop, and in the window was a pair of glasses that reminded me of his. I became unglued. I just sat there in the car, crying so hard I couldn't tell my friends what was wrong."

What was wrong was simply life — random, bittersweet, heartbreaking life. But always worth living.

17

'CAUSE YOU'VE GOT
HIGH HOPES

Once you get through the waves of grief, it's time to start concentrating on living in the present. A few years ago, I clipped this little poem from a newspaper:

Yesterday is history,
Tomorrow is a mystery.
Today is a gift.
That's why it's called the present.

It may not be Wordsworth or even Hallmark, but it's wise. In a way you have no choice: The present is your permanent address.

When someone once asked Yogi Berra, the great New York Yankee, for the time, he said, "You mean right now?"

Yogi must have had in mind all the people whose watches are set to earlier years. He also must have known that those people are always unhappy, no matter how pleasant the past might have been. I have always felt that the biggest obstacle to happiness is letting your longing for the past block your appreciation for the present and your enthusiasm for the future.

Even though the time *is* always right now (I think I got that from Einstein, or Alex

Trebek), the best way to stay enthusiastic about the future is to set long-range goals that force you to stretch yourself and see how much you can achieve. Dream big, and don't hate yourself if you fall on your face. As Robert Browning wrote:

> *. . . a man's dreams should exceed*
> *his grasp,*
> *Or what's a heaven for?*

Or, as my grandmother, who was never anthologized, used to put it, "You should always want. It keeps you on your toes."

I like the answer of the writer who was asked, "Of all your books, which one do you think is the best?"

"The one I'm writing now," he replied.

Artie Shaw, probably the greatest band clarinetist of the century, was known to be very hard on his own work because he kept feeling he could do better.

"Is there any recording of yours that you're satisfied with?" a critic once asked him.

"Well," said Shaw, "there are a couple of bars of 'Begin the Beguine' that are all right."

You don't have to be *that* hard on yourself, but you do have to keep striving. I am constantly updating my list of goals, which you should have at every age. When Leonard

Bernstein was sixty-seven, he told a reporter, "I feel as though I've just begun."

A few years ago I had my own talk about the future with a magazine writer.

"Is there anything left you want to accomplish?" she'd asked me.

Ten minutes later she interrupted my answer and said with a laugh, "*Please*, Joan, enough!" And I hadn't even gotten to my desire to be a centerfold for *Modern Maturity*.

Without something to strive for, our lives become meaningless. So many retirees die soon after they stop working: When they retired from a job, they didn't realize that they also quit life. The most miserable people I know aren't those who have to work two jobs to pay the rent, but those who can't think of a single thing they still want to achieve. And a stock dividend doesn't count. Some of the richest people who ever lived — for example, Doris Duke and J. Paul Getty — led lives that could only be called impoverished. In fact a 1996 *Forbes* survey of America's one hundred wealthiest people found that they were not fundamentally happier than the working class.

Believe it or not, even winning the lottery doesn't guarantee happiness, for many lottery winners have admitted being unhappy. Some have lost good friends, and some have been bothered by the thought that they had no control over winning the money. Our Puritan heritage is hard to escape — mine goes back to Cotton Katz — but there is something unsatisfying about getting money you didn't work for; earning the money is much more rewarding.

During World War II one commanding officer had this credo for his men: "The hard way is the best way. Not because it is the best way. But because it is the hard way."

Even animals need challenges and goals. Last year Gus, a polar bear at the Central Park Zoo, began to sit listlessly in the water, never moving or playing with the other bears. An animal psychiatrist found that Gus's problem was too much time on his hands and too little to work for. Well fed and pampered, Gus had no need to feed or protect himself. When the zookeeper started hiding Gus's food and Gus had to hunt for it, his depression quickly disappeared. One of his new goals was probably to eat the zookeeper.

As you bounce back from a crisis, you may decide that you liked your life just as it was before disaster struck, that you would like to re-create that life as well as you can. Many people have shared this feeling with me.

"It may not sound like the loftiest goal,"

says a woman named Robin, "but my objective after Marty went to jail was just to keep my apartment and not have to live on a smaller scale. With that in mind, I worked hard, studied hard, and focused on finishing school and getting a good job."

And a woman named Nancy, who was diagnosed with bone cancer before her freshman year of college, says, "I had been perfectly happy with my life before I got sick, and I had a lot of plans: go abroad my junior year, graduate from college, and go to law school. All those old goals were important to me, and I decided I wanted to achieve them despite the time I had to take off for the operation and the treatments."

In examining my own life after Edgar died, I decided — just as Robin and Nancy did — that there was much of my old existence that I wanted to restore. I wanted to get back into show business and start performing; and I wanted to start going out and become part of a couple again. The prospect of dating was scary, of course, for I knew the rules had changed. Did a man today bring you flowers or his blood test report on the first date?

There were also parts of my life that I wanted to change. A major one was deciding to move to New York City; and I knew that moving would mean making new friends. During our marriage Edgar and I had spent a lot of time with *his* friends, European intellectuals who didn't always share my sense of fun. A German sense of humor is an oxymoron. And so, I decided that when I moved to New York, I would build a social life around people who made *me* feel comfortable.

"The aftermath of a major loss or crisis is an ideal time to give yourself permission to try something new or even something that seems crazy," says Dr. Silver Bigelson. "Many people will urge you to get back to the familiar; but before you stumble down the path of least resistance, take some time to think about what you really want. You may be surprised to discover that what you want after a crisis is very different from what you'd wanted just a few months before."

Yes, loss may force you to realize that you have talents you haven't been using and interests beyond the ones you've explored.

"After my husband died," says Sheila, "I realized that I had always tailored myself to his habits in so many little ways that I now was living a life very different from the one I had dreamed of. I loved my husband enormously, but I also had put him and the kids first. Well, now it was my turn, and I set out to recapture some of the dreams I'd had when I was younger.

"For example, I'd always wanted to be a writer, but Allen and I had gotten married when I was finishing college; and in those days, having and raising children came first. I also had always wanted to take really adventurous vacations, but Allen liked tamer ones. So I got brochures on writing courses at the local community college and brochures on adventurous vacations, for I'd had a wonderful time alone in Paris and now knew I could travel anywhere by myself. I slowly got back in touch with what I enjoyed and wanted. I began to feel that the rest of my life wasn't going to be an afterthought but a whole new adventure."

"There are no second acts in American lives," said F. Scott Fitzgerald. He was wrong. In fact, Fitzgerald himself had a second act after the mental breakdown of his beloved Zelda and his own crackup: He became a Hollywood screenwriter and also found a new love.

And what a second act Nancy Archuleta staged for herself! At fifteen she was a poor, pregnant, high school dropout. Then her misery had a change of pace. After a rotten marriage she fled with her four children, juggled several jobs, and finished her education. Today Nancy is chairman and CEO of MEVATEC, a multimillion-dollar software business that's one of America's fastest-growing Hispanic-owned companies. That's a second act that rates a few curtain calls.

Thrilling second acts, in fact, are now common for American women, who are bouncing back from hardship like the spaldeens of my girlhood, the pink rubber balls that filled the skies of New York in the forties and fifties. Look at Judith Dignon and Gayle Martz.

At twenty-three Judith Dignon was in a car accident that killed her husband and broke her back. That seemed like an ideal time for her to give up. Instead, after years of physical therapy and pain, she found a new career in the traffic safety industry (once dominated by men) and now is CEO of the booming American Barricade, Inc.

Gayle Martz had just lost her job as a flight attendant when she awoke one morning to find that her fiancé had died in his sleep. To make things even merrier for Gayle, his will wasn't signed and she found herself with no home, no money, and no job — the triple crown.

Gayle felt she had hit rock bottom; her

only comfort was her dog; she began to take it everywhere. But suddenly, the dog became more than comfort: It was the idea for a new business. Gayle designed a soft-sided pet carrier that allowed small animals to travel next to their owners instead of in cargo holds — and then she spent years persuading airlines to let these carriers on. Today, almost all airlines accept her product, which is made by the Sherpa's Pet Trading Company: Its president is Gayle Martz.

Another inspiring second act is the one that C. Z. Guest has had. Her first was being the wife of a wealthy and prominent man, a full-time job: Day and night she dealt with kids, florists, caterers, and parties. However, after her husband died, she found herself not only widowed but "unemployed," for her employment had been the traditional unpaid slavery of the American woman: wife, a job that wouldn't exactly shine on a résumé.

"So tell me, Mrs. Guest, how many positions did you have as a wife? Do you have any references?"

Because she had always liked gardening, C.Z. started to write a column about plants for a Long Island newspaper, a column that grew so popular that it was soon running in newspapers across the United States. Today, in her seventies, she is a businesswoman who sells tulip bulbs by mail and has her own brand of fertilizer. Many people in television have their own brands of fertilizer, but only C.Z.'s has helped America bloom, and has let C.Z. bloom as well. She has triumphantly discovered that there was always more to her than just being a wife.

"When Winston died," she says, "I decided to change my life for my own salvation. You *can't* lead the same life all the time."

No matter how old you are, how many false starts you've made, or how many blows you've been dealt, you still can re-create your life the way that C. Z. Guest, Nancy Archuleta, Gayle Martz, and Judith Dignon did. You can even bounce back from an unsuccessful term as President of the United States.

Jimmy Carter's second act didn't equal Winston Churchill's — none ever has — but it may be the best second act in American public life. Because of the Iranian hostage crisis and other bungles, Carter left the White House in near disgrace. In the years since then, however, he has become perhaps the most successful and respected ex-president in American history. He has been a diplomat; he has been a peacemaker; he helps to run Habitat for Humanity, an organization that builds homes for the indigent; and he has even published a book of poetry.

My own fiancé, Orin Lehman, is another fine example of the resilience of the human spirit, of how a life can be splendidly rebuilt. In 1940 Orin was at Princeton, where he played football, polo, tennis, and starred on the track team. He once told me that if he'd been asked in his twenties to choose between sports and sex, he would have taken the track instead of the sack. (I used to make other guys feel the same way.)

And then World War II broke out. Orin enlisted and lost a leg in Germany. However, instead of feeling sorry for himself, he came home, earned a Ph.D., and became the head of New York's New School for Social Research. On one leg and crutches, he marched with Martin Luther King, Jr. He ran for New York City controller and won; and then he became the New York State commissioner of parks and recreation for twenty-three years.

But there was one more thing: Orin had to see if there was a sport that he could still play. And there was. When I watch him hit a golf ball as he balances on one leg, I tingle with the thought that the human spirit is unconquerable. Orin and those bounce-back women and so many others I've talked to at lectures are all the children of Churchill. Every one of them has said: "Never, never, never give up."

"Either you vegetate and look out the window or activate and try to effect change," says Christopher Reeve, who is planning to walk within seven years. Now he is truly Superman.

And so, as you're bouncing back, ask yourself: What do I really want out of life? And write the answer down.

You've probably decided that you want a wonderful social life, a successful career, fabulous looks, and a marvelous relationship with one special person; but those are vague wishes, not concrete goals. Your goals have to be specific:

I want to write advertising copy.
I want to lose twenty pounds.
I want to meet an attractive plastic surgeon.

A poll of Yale's Class of 1953 revealed that only 3 percent of the graduates had set concrete goals for themselves at the age of twenty-two. The other 97 percent had left college with just vague expectations of success and happiness. Twenty years later the 3 percent who'd set goals were earning more money than the entire other 97 percent of the class!

Of course, high income is not the only measure of success, but the imbalance in those alumni earnings reflects a truth about every facet of life: The more specific your goal, the more likely you are to achieve it. For example, a young man named Bill Clinton wanted to be president in the worst way. (And that's how he's done it, the Republicans say.) The presidency and nothing else was the focus of all his attention, his energy, and his desire.

If a great social life is at the top of your list, precisely what does that mean? Dozens of friends you occasionally see and lie to? One truly close friend who becomes your soul mate? A romantic involvement with a man who can read your mind and melt your heart? A baby by Prince Charles?

"I decided that I needed to take a break from dating for a while," says Paula, who left her lover, Mitchell, after seven years. "I suddenly wanted to have a lot of different and interesting friends, people of all ages and backgrounds, people involved in a wide range of activities, so there's always something new to talk about and learn about."

Brenda's social goal, however, is quite different: "I want to trust a man long enough to enter a long, intimate relationship," she says, an admirable aim for a survivor of childhood sexual abuse.

You can't let *anything* in your past stop you from moving ahead. You were abused when you were six? You're forty-one now — time to get over it and move on.

Be as specific as you can about your social goals — and your other goals, too. What does success mean to you? Helping battered children? Becoming a corporate vice-president? Working nine-to-five so you have time for outside interests or having a job you enjoy so much that you don't mind working till ten or eleven every night? Of course, with a job like that, you'll have the social life of a mother superior, so understand that going in.

Also think about your spare time, what new skills or hobbies you want to learn. In *The Psychology of Happiness*, Michael Fordyce says: "Happy individuals have many sources of happiness. When your happiness depends on one thing or one person, you're on shaky ground."

Things might have worked out for Othello if he'd had a pastime besides Desdemona.

"A diverse identity will save you if you're having trouble in any one area of your life," says Dr. Georgia Witkin, a psychotherapist. "If things are lousy at the office, you're less likely to feel hopeless if you're also a mother or a lover or a great tennis player."

When you make your list of things that you believe could make you happy, you may find more than one dream in each category. For instance, you may want to be a surgeon *and* a concert pianist. You probably can't name too many of those, someone who might be fixing a hernia in three-quarter time, but it's all right to let your fantasies fly. Of course, a surgeon who's also a concert pianist is liable to have his beeper go off during Brahms.

Do you want to be an astronaut and a ballerina? Do you want to dance *Swan Lake* on the moon? Then take a shot. As Bing Crosby nicely put it in one of his films:

Oh, there's nothing to be ashamed of
If you stub your toe on the moon.

If you're having trouble coming up with any buried dreams, then ask yourself: If you won the lottery tomorrow, how would you spend the money? On a trip around the world? If so, consider doing some traveling in your nonfantasy life. Would you give a big hunk of your winnings to the local zoo? Then consider going to work at a pet store or simply getting a pet of your own. Or would you buy municipal bonds?

Another way to learn about your interests is to see which section of the Sunday paper you turn to first and which will be first to line the birdcage? Business? News of the Week? Arts and Leisure? Real Estate? Style?

"After Steve left," says Betty, "it struck me that I always turned first to the real estate section to see the layouts in the ads for new condos. I have a real fascination with space and decorating, and so, when I needed to work after my divorce, I decided to be an interior designer."

Once you've trimmed your list to lofty but still attainable goals, you have to ask yourself: What is the cost of pursuing this goal? If you decide you'd rather be a neurosurgeon than a crossing guard, you'll need eight years of training at high annual tuition; and if you want to run a marathon, you'll need just as much training and a high threshold of pain.

Dream big but be realistic; sometimes one goal will displace another. You can't sing opera professionally and also be a lawyer unless you plan to have no clients; there simply isn't time for both; and it's almost impossible to renovate a house *and* learn Chinese. If you want to know Chinese and renovate a house, you'd better *be* Chinese. Nevertheless, in spite of the all-or-nothing philosophy that many of us have, it's all right to do a couple of things imperfectly, if that blend will make you happy. Learn a little Chinese and renovate just one room at a time.

Too many of us are locked into the all-or-nothing approach. We say: I'm never going to get that Ph.D., so why bother even going back for my bachelor's? If my genes say I'll never be a size four, then I may as well forget about size four jeans and just keep eating. This attitude, however, keeps you from taking that vital first step. As the Chinese say (even if you read this in English), The journey of ten thousand miles begins with a single step.

Once your goal list is trimmed, do not be stopped by the fear of failure, criticism, or ridicule. Remember Ira Gershwin's line, "They all laughed at Christopher Columbus"? People must even have laughed at the man who invented the wheel.

"But what can you *do* with it?" they may have said.

"Make pizzas," the inventor could have replied.

"Don't be stupid; pizzas are *square*."

Failure, although painful, can in fact lead to new chances. Would I ever have thought of going into the jewelry business in the early 1990s if my show business career had been booming? And what was my training? Making shell necklaces when I was six at the beach. However, a passion for something can make up for a lack of formal education; and if you find that you do need the education, then go out and get it, no matter how long you've been out of school.

"You can't wake up one day and start writing for a newspaper," says Sheila. "So I knew I had to take some courses. At first I was ready to give up because I figured out that by the time I was ready to start writing professionally, I'd be sixty-three. And then I realized that even if I didn't go to school, I'd still turn sixty-three on exactly the same date."

The biggest obstacle to your success is often not the degrees or knowledge you lack but what you *think* you can't achieve. You tell yourself: I'm too dumb, too fat, too shy, too unsophisticated. And you reminisce about every insult you've ever heard. And so, to banish the negative thoughts, you've got to tell yourself how wonderful you are. It might not have worked for

Bonnie and Clyde, but it *will* work for you. Make a list of everything you're good at and read it aloud at least once every day, being very sure that nobody hears you. But definitely listen to *yourself.*

Write down not only your strengths but also memorable compliments that people give you. Such a double list can let you dispel self-doubts and will your way to good things. In *Success Is Not an Accident,* Dr. John Kappas says that handwriting bypasses the conscious mind and implants ideas directly into the powerful subconscious, the best first step in changing your life. This is not Toad's list of how to spend the day: This is using your central nervous system to get yourself launched, for when you write something down, you are defeating resistance in three ways: You are thinking about what you're writing, you are physically writing it, and you are seeing it as you write.

All of us grow up with labels and expectations that are often foolish or untrue. Maybe you were the "difficult" sister, or maybe, like me, you were the "fat and shy" one. Removing those labels is supremely important, the way that Alec Guinness removed his label of "no actor," and Fred Astaire removed "Dances a little."

You'd be amazed how many seemingly

237

confident people have had to give themselves pep talks. Many years ago I asked Laurence Olivier if he ever suffered from stage fright.

"I have to give myself a little speech," he replied. "I look out at the stage and I say to myself, 'That is my space. All of that space. I deserve to be there. No one else fills it the way that I do.' "

That was one of the reasons he was Laurence Olivier. Another was a hell of a lot of talent.

Whether you are walking out to play *Hamlet* or to begin a journey of self-discovery, the pictures in your mind have the power to make things happen. For example, professional athletes often visualize themselves moving to victory. I still get a thrill thinking about how Joe Namath, the great quarterback of the New York Jets, used such positive thinking in the 1969 Super Bowl. Going into that game, Namath's Jets were seventeen-point underdogs to the mighty Baltimore Colts. Just one factor hadn't been considered: Namath had decided that the Jets weren't going to lose.

"I guarantee we'll win," he had said before the game.

People laughed at his boast. Yes, the same laughter was used for Columbus and the guy who tried to patent the wheel. At the end of the game, Namath was cheered from coast to coast for leading such an upset, but it had been no upset to him. It was simply a plan he had made.

A famous golfer once said that before each swing, he took a moment to practice in the theater of the mind: He mentally saw the perfect swing and its results. Of course, such theater of the mind alone won't make all your dreams come true; I'm sure that Susan Lucci keeps picturing herself accepting an Emmy. The theater of the mind simply means that you are aiming as high as you can.

"If you aim for the stars," my grandmother used to say, "you'll land on the roof. But if you just aim for the roof, you'll land in the cellar."

It probably sounded better in Russian. But my grandmother knew that we often fall short of our dreams. She knew that we don't have to accomplish everything. In fact, the act of working toward a goal can be as rewarding as reaching it. Remember what I said about a writer always having the fun of the writing, whether or not the work is produced? Well, J. D. Salinger hasn't had a word published since 1965, but he hasn't stopped writing: He has been producing new prose and enjoying it.

"There is enormous pleasure in writing not for publication," he says.

It's a pleasure that certain critics should explore.

18

ONE SMALL STEP FOR YOU, ONE GIANT STEP, TOO

My bumblebee pin is my second favorite piece of jewelry. My favorite piece is a pin that Edgar gave me: a little diamond turtle with its head sticking way out.

"This is how you've lived your life, Joan," he said. "The turtle can't move unless it sticks out its neck. And you've always stuck out *your* neck and taken trudging little steps to get where you're going."

Slow and steady won't do much for your bet in the daily double, but it's the way to win the race of your life. From the beginning of my career, I've kept moving ahead in measured little steps, never taking my eye off the goal, in spite of the three R's: resistance, ridicule, and rejection.

First I had to find myself, perhaps in response to all the producers who said "Get lost." You see, in the beginning, I didn't want to be a comedienne: I wanted to be an actress. I went to agent after agent; and each one watched me perform and then responded with a heartfelt, "Forget it." They told me I had everything needed to be a star, except for looks and talent.

After hearing such moving responses, I would wander back to the receptionist and make jokes to cover the hurt I was feeling.

And the receptionists began to tell their bosses that I was funny. At last one of the agents told me, "Joan, I'll never send you out as an actress — not if I want to stay in this business — but there's a chance I could get you something at a little stand-up comedy club."

I considered his offer for three or four seconds and accepted it. At that little club, which had all the theatrical chic of a Texaco station, I began to try out my jokes and hone them until they got laughs in the right places. Slowly, over many years, I moved on to bigger agents and bigger jobs. I was not exactly an overnight sensation, but almost no one ever is. The exceptions are so few and so memorable: Barbra Streisand exploding from nowhere in the Broadway musical, *I Can Get It for You Wholesale*; Carol Burnett enchanting a nation of TV viewers with the hilarious song, "I Made a Fool of Myself Over John Foster Dulles"; Leonard Bernstein's burst of genius as a substitute conductor at Carnegie Hall; Shirley Temple in her first film; and the Beatles on *The Ed Sullivan Show*.

But that's not the way it's usually done. Most careers are like Elmore Leonard's: writing book after book in obscurity until one of them, *Glitz*, was finally a hit.

In the early days, my goal was a simple one: to be an international star, to entertain the entire earth, though I wasn't sure how I'd go over in Iraq once they learned I was Jewish. True to the Chinese saying, my journey of ten thousand miles had begun with small steps.

I reminded myself of those steps after Edgar's suicide; and three years ago, during my professional and personal lows, I reminded myself of them again. At both times the big-dreams/small-steps approach had worked for me. No matter how defeated you feel, no matter how tired and dismayed, never lose sight of your goal and never stop thinking of ways to reach it. Keep thinking of life as that paneled room and keep pushing all the boards until one turns into a door and swings open. It'll be a small door, so you'd better be watching your weight because you *must* go through it.

After Edgar's death, when nighttime television shows and big nightclubs had suddenly never heard of me, I forced myself to work on *Hollywood Squares* and in the tiniest comedy clubs. I couldn't allow myself the luxury of feeling humiliated, just as Patti LuPone couldn't waste time nurturing humiliation after Andrew Lloyd Webber had fired her from *Sunset Boulevard*. (She eventually returned to rave reviews as Maria Callas in Broadway's *Master Class*.) Working on *Hollywood Squares* and in tiny clubs kept me busy and helped build my confidence to take bigger steps and make bolder moves.

In early 1988 I read in the *New York Times* that Manny Azenberg, a major producer, was planning to start a repertory company at Lincoln Center. A few years earlier, I had met Manny when he was recasting *The Odd Couple* with women instead of men, and he had offered me one of the leading roles. After reading this *Times* story, I called him and asked him to keep me in mind if any parts came up that I could play. At this point I was so determined to bounce back that I felt I could play Lady Macbeth, if the audience would simply accept that she had a New York accent.

A few weeks later, Manny told me that there was a part open in his new production of Neil Simon's *Broadway Bound*. At once, I flew to New York, watched the play, and was enraptured. The part was a gem, and I felt the way Sinatra had when discovering Maggio in *From Here to Eternity*: The part had been custom made for me. Kate Jerome was a mother who had tried to do everything right for her family and still had lost them all in the space of just a few months.

"I'd *love* to do the part," I told Manny.

"You'll have to read for it," he said.

Once they reach a certain level of fame, many performers will not audition, but that kind of misplaced pride had never been mine, just as it hadn't been Judy Holliday's — and she was as big as a star could be. And so I read for Manny and Gene Saks, the director; and the moment I had finished, they offered me the part. Twenty-five years had passed since I had tried to push my way into the offices of agents. At last I was literally *Broadway Bound*!

To get the part right, I now worked harder than I had ever done. Every night until the wee hours, I went over my lines at home. My taking a Broadway role would have a lot of people looking hard at me. When opening night finally came, my nerves were raw.

In the *New York Post*, Clive Barnes's review contained a thought that I don't think was ever expressed about Geraldine Page: "The audience was not expecting much," he wrote. He went on to say, however, "Rivers is beautifully truthful and touching." And the rest of his review was a valentine to my performance! I was dazzled to see the other New York papers give the same opinion, one that even I, the big dreamer, had never allowed to addle my brain. I had never planned to be Helen Hayes; Gabby Hayes had seemed more my style. Nevertheless it was true: Joan Molinsky, the loser of Larchmont, had become a Broadway star.

Once I saw how much the critics and the audiences liked me, my confidence grew Napoleonic. And when *Broadway Bound* finally closed, I was ready to conquer other parts of the show business world. Comedy clubs all over the country began to book me again, and soon I was welcomed back to Las Vegas. The dead duck was a phoenix once more.

Although I was thoroughly enjoying all the work and the gratifying responses, something was still missing: I missed interviewing people. Not long after I'd been struck by this thought, my agent called with an offer from the Tribune Corporation to host a syndicated daytime television show. When I had a meeting with the Tribune people, we found a rapport. There was none of the hostility that had been a fundamental part of my relationship with Fox. I agreed to do the show and went on the air with delight.

For the next six years, *The Joan Rivers Show* was my happy home. It gave me a place to do the kind of television I had always done best: freewheeling comic monologues and exchanges with people that ranged from the funny to the deeply felt. I was working again,

I was laughing again, and I felt wondrously worthwhile.

In 1990 this rewarding life peaked with my nomination for an Emmy. All during the ceremony, as I waited for the show to reach my category, I tried to keep my hopes realistic.

Just being nominated is enough, I told myself. It doesn't matter if you win.

You're full of baloney, myself replied.

Just being nominated might have been good enough for Geraldine Ferraro, but it wasn't good enough for me. It mattered like *hell* if I won! And the power of the theater of the mind worked for me: My name was suddenly called out as the winner of the Emmy for best talk-show host. The rush of joy that I felt was stronger than any I had known in years.

At the podium I accepted my award and then held it high in triumph, the way Wimbledon winners often did. And in my elation, I thought of Edgar and how proud he would have been at the distance I had come, both professionally and personally, in the three years since his suicide. I reminded myself that even though life is governed by accidents, this hadn't been one: This bouncing back had been endless hard work and no misplaced pride. Not once had I said, "I'll take only work that will get me an Emmy." Instead I had said, "I'll take any work I can get and do whatever I have to do to survive." And I did that work with little steps, just like the turtle that Edgar had known I was. There is no other way to rebuild a career — or a life.

In bouncing back you have to take one challenge at a time, moving ahead like the turtle: with a steady pace and a very thick hide.

The steady advancing of a turtle was the style that Meghan used to get back the money her husband had stolen from her.

"I hired a fabulous lawyer," she says, "and took Bob to court. I had to do a ton of work to prove all the things that were mine, to prove that he had taken my rightful money. It involved a lot of time and pain; but in the end I got back every cent I deserved. And I took control of my life by refusing to let Bob and his lawyers intimidate me."

I applaud her spunk; I've spent plenty of time with lawyers, too, in my fight to regain control of Joan Rivers Products. It took two years of negotiations and battles. I went to every meeting myself and read every word of the jargon that lawyers use instead of English.

At one meeting I got so angry at one of

the opposing lawyers that I took off a heavy earring and flung it at him, a fitting way to make a point in an argument about jewelry. (He was lucky we weren't fighting about a knife company.) When I launched that particular piece of jewelry at that particular son of a bitch, everyone in the room was shocked, for they weren't used to seeing such behavior in a business conference; but I was frustrated and exhausted. For two years I'd been waking up in the middle of the night afraid that I would never reach an agreement with the bondholders, and that I would end up still owing thirty-seven million dollars, plus the staggering legal fees.

At last, in the fall of 1995, my persistence and my lawyers' hard work paid off: I got my business and my name back for a part of the original debt that had been oppressing me. And now, if I make my business as successful as it can be and if I live to be 126, I have a chance to pay off what I still owe.

All the while that I was fighting to regain control of Joan Rivers Products, I was in another battle, too. After *Sally Marr* closed, I was deeply depressed. However, just as I had done after Fox had canceled my show, I said to Dorothy, "Let's get on the phone *now* and start setting up meetings with anyone we think might have work for me. Let's do everything we can to get me jobs."

Because the nighttime shows like Leno and Letterman were still refusing to book me (it was now seven years!), I looked in other directions and found new homes on shows like *Politically Incorrect*, Howard Stern, *Regis and Kathie Lee*, and Conan O'Brien. Jumping all over the channels, I was also guest host on *Larry King* and *Good Morning America*. I began to regain confidence in my ability to bounce back. As always I knew that yet again I had to be willing to start small.

For several years Don Rickles had been asking me to costar with him, and I had always said no: I had feared that if he and I were together on one bill, the audience would overdose on a mix of comedy that was too rich. Each of us had a strong, distinctive voice that needed to be complemented by a softer tone.

This time, however, when Don Rickles came with his offer, I said the hell with my theory of how to blend comedy, and I hit the road with him. Just as the Three Tenors have worked out musically, so did the Two Mad Mouths comedically. Although I no longer wanted to tour endlessly, I realized that touring is what I would have to do if I wanted to keep working.

And so I went on the road with Don and

had a wonderful time: Audiences adored the pairing, and our double bill worked hilariously. And what also began to work was my telephone — with calls from someone other than lawyers.

In 1994 E!, the Entertainment Network, called and asked me to do the preawards show for the Golden Globes. At first, I was reluctant to say yes because, at that time, few people had heard of the new network. However, once again, it was work and the work that let me try to be at my best. I knew I had always been a natural on TV, and I desperately missed doing it. Therefore I decided to meet with E!'s executives, who turned out to be savvy and enthusiastic people.

"You can do anything you want," they told me. "No holds barred."

No holds barred? Those happen to be my three favorite words in the English language, except perhaps for "*You're* over fifty?"

Doing that preawards show turned out to be another marvelous move. I was playing through my strength, ad-libbing good cracks about the stars, their sex lives, and their clothes. The show received a very high rating, and the network asked me to consider more hosting; and they also asked me to consider using a cohost named Melissa Rivers. Since I knew the young woman's work

— from her first finger painting, in fact — I accepted with delight.

The first show that Melissa and I did together for E! was the Academy Awards of 1995. With Melissa on one end of the runway and her mother on the other, the two of us interviewed the nominees as they walked in. We kept throwing the talk back and forth to each other; and for the first time in my career, I wasn't bothered that my costar was younger, prettier, and sexier. I was too busy being consumed by pride.

In the two years since that Oscar show, Melissa and I, the Jewish Judds, have done many more awards and fashion shows for E!; and all of them have brought the highest ratings ever received by this suddenly hot and very watchable channel.

This little step-by-step style is also the way that I rebuilt my social life. After Edgar died I knew that I wanted to start dating again, because I missed the feeling of belonging with someone. I missed the pleasure of sharing the silly details of my day with someone who actually cared how that day had been. I missed the comfort of having someone to kiss my forehead when I was sick or someone whom *I* could take care of when he was sick or down. Some anthropologist once said that one of humanity's strongest needs is to know that there is someone who cares whether you've come safely home.

And equally sweet is having someone to make the trip with you. As a song in *The Golden Apple* — a 1954 musical based on Greek mythology — perfectly says:

It's the goin' home together
When the day is done.

But *dating?* When the Marine Corps refers to "a few good men," it is also referring to what's available to a suddenly single woman. *Dating?* After twenty-two years of marriage, I had no idea how to start. The last time I'd been dating, I used to ask the guy, "What's your major?" However, when you're over fifty, if you ask a guy where he went to college, he may not remember.

Nevertheless, I began to meet a few single men. Although none seemed right, I began to accept their invitations, reminding myself that I wasn't going on dates to have a great time. I was going on dates to meet someone I liked well enough so I could *stop* going on dates.

In spite of this somewhat unromantic approach, I was surprised to discover that, even in middle age, even after twenty-two years of marriage, I still got crushes. I found myself nervously waiting for phone calls. I found myself trying on forty-six different dresses before each dinner date. In the restaurant, I would wonder: Am I talking too much? Am I talking enough? Am I being charming? Am I being too loud?

In my first few months as a single woman, I felt awkwardness and disappointment and I even shed a few tears. But whenever I thought of giving up, I also thought how nice it would be to have someone with whom I could share a midnight snack in the kitchen.

In the fall following Edgar's death, I encountered some nice men at business meetings in New York; and when I was looking for an apartment there, I met a real estate mogul who was both charming and funny. Although we became good friends, I wasn't in love with him. The problem for him and me wasn't the wit, it was the fit: Our styles and priorities were simply too different. Nevertheless, I will always be grateful that my first beau after Edgar's death was a man whose warmth eased my way back into the scary world of old-boy-meets-old-girl.

My next romance, however, was one that made me wonder if there was something else a girl could meet. I met a man who instantly impressed me with his culture and polish, but as the months went by, I discovered that he had neither generosity nor warmth. Cheap and cold is not a combination that Jerome Kern wrote about.

One night at a dinner party, after this man had ignored half my friends and insulted some others, I looked in the mirror and said to myself, Joan, you could get this from Don Rickles, but there would be laughs. It's better to be by yourself than to be with someone who's going to make you angry all the time. Although it was nice to have an escort, someone with whom I could take a walk in the park, it was better to go it alone than to be in the company of a man who felt that having a heart was optional.

After I sailed away from this iceberg, I spent many months dining out with groups of my girlfriends. I knew that I could live alone for as long as I had to. And then, as if rewarding my self-sufficiency, the gods sent me a very special man named Orin Lehman, who is kind, witty, generous, and loving.

"When Orin and Joan are together," says my old friend Tom Corcoran, "and they're always laughing and joking, I look at him sometimes and he is just beaming."

Your first relationships after the loss of a love may not be successful, but those early, groping tries will slowly move you toward the sweet permanence that you deserve.

"Soon after the divorce," says Meghan, "I wanted to start dating again, but I wasn't quite ready for an intense relationship. I met a really great guy who lived in Nashville, and for a while we had a long-distance romance. It felt good to know there'd be men interested in me again. After that fizzled out, I had a few short-term things with guys here in Chicago and finally I got into a serious, long-term thing."

In easing our way out of despair, it would be nice, of course, if we could have those first three or four men lined up at once and say, "Bachelor number two: Are you a son of a bitch?" But risk and pain are always involved. Every enterprise in life is a roll of the dice; but meeting the right person sometimes seems not quite as easy as winning the lottery.

"After Mitchell and I broke up," says Paula, "I realized how many friendships I'd let slide during my seven years with him. I was very lonely, but I felt awkward calling up people I hadn't seen in ages and saying, 'Hi, remember me?' So I set out to make new friends. I took a history class at the university and a lecture series at a local church. And I started asking people in my office to come to my house for dinner — not just people I knew well but semistrangers too. So I made some close friends and had some interesting evenings with people I never would have met if I hadn't stuck my neck out."

Once again the voice of the turtle is heard in the land, and it's a voice of justified self-satisfaction.

"My neighbors in Boca didn't know me that well before my husband died," says Sheila, "so when I became this very gutsy woman, they weren't surprised; they had nothing to compare me to. But when I went north for the holidays, my old friends had trouble accepting the new me. Even after I'd told them I was taking writing courses, wilderness vacations, and yoga classes, they still just asked me about the kids and tennis. I wanted to scream, 'Can't you *see?* I'm a *new person!*' "

Americans don't mind if you're born again religiously, but a professional or social rebirth seems to give them trouble. The changes in my own life have made some of my old friends uneasy. My moving boldly in new directions has made some of them wonder: Whatever happened to the old Joan? Have they been witnessing some kind of "Three Faces of Joan"?

If Edgar returned today, *he* wouldn't recognize me. His Joan now living in New York, lecturing on survival, playing golf, and running a prosperous jewelry business? The woman who couldn't find the checkbook? And if she had found it, she might have used the checks for bookmarks.

As passionately as Darwin did, I now believe in evolution. Edgar's wife was a comedian and nothing else; but my life in the last three years has taught me that *anything* is possible if you refuse to let yourself be stopped by the size of the challenges you face and instead break them into small, conquerable ones.

That's how a couple named Alex and Kim set about adopting a daughter.

"I became very organized," says Kim. "I went to the library and read everything I could about foreign adoption, and I surfed the Internet to talk to people around the world who'd adopted babies from other countries. We also got a lawyer and talked to agencies that could put us in touch with foreign orphanages. Finally, we decided to try and adopt a baby girl from China.

"It was a huge project, much bigger than I'd ever imagined.

"At last, we flew to China, spent five days nursing our new baby through an ear infection, and then brought her home. I was so overwhelmed that I cried on and off for days."

At times being a mother has been overwhelming for me too. And restoring my relationship with Melissa after Edgar's death was a long and often agonizing process for me. By the time she returned to college for her senior year, we were enjoying each other's company; and when graduation neared, she told me that her classmates wanted me to speak at the ceremony. At first the invitation delighted me. But then I thought: I don't want to turn this into "Commencement Starring Joan Rivers."

"I'm very flattered," I told Melissa, "but I think I shouldn't. This is your moment, and I don't want to steal it from you."

"Mom," she said warmly, "even if you just sat in the balcony, the spotlight would still be on you. It would mean a *lot* to me if you spoke."

And so I addressed her college graduating class of the University of Pennsylvania. I told a few jokes and gave the graduates the usual commencement advice. But there was nothing usual about the way I felt on that graduation day. My daughter had been through more pain in two years than any woman deserves in a lifetime, and she had come through. Not only had she graduated with her class on time, but she had graduated with honors. Even more important, she had retained her kind and sensitive heart.

When I finished my speech, I looked into the audience and saw Melissa and the friends who had helped her through the last two years. Few events on earth are more moving than a college graduation. Melissa and her friends looked so brave and confident as they prepared to head into the big scary world. And I knew that waiting for them were sharks that belonged in *Jaws*. These kids would need so much courage and luck. They would have to be a new batch of Winston Churchill's disciples. I hoped that some of them were aware that *I* had never given up.

"I love you, Melissa," I suddenly said, as if the two of us were alone, and she answered by blowing me a kiss from her seat. I was so overwhelmed by joy and pride and relief that we had found our way back to each other that I could barely hold myself together long enough to leave the podium.

And then the entire class rose and gave me a standing ovation. My stand-up career should have ended right there, for knocking 'em dead at Buckingham Palace would have been just a lounge act compared to this. Of course, this was the first applause I'd ever gotten that wasn't really for me. It was for my daughter.

When Melissa moved to California to look for a job in television, I knew that we would always stay close, no matter what life threw at us. We both had worked too hard to rebuild our relationship, and we knew we would never let it fall apart again. We knew the truth of what Spencer Tracy had quoted in *Father of the Bride*: "Your son is your son till he takes him a wife, but your daughter's your daughter for all of your life."

In 1995 Melissa and I decided to make a movie together: *Tears and Laughter: The Joan and Melissa Rivers Story*. Yes, we told the incredulous interviewers, we were going to make a movie about Edgar's suicide and its aftermath. And yes, we were going to play ourselves. Who *else* would play us: Cher and Tori Spelling?

The acting itself was healing for us. Enough time had passed so that Melissa the actress could display only cinematic passion when she cried, "I hate you, Mother! I've been invisible to you ever since Daddy died!" Now, looking back, she could imagine how I must have felt when we'd played that scene for an audience of two. And when I got to shout back at her all over again, I felt as though the hurt had left my system forever.

Moreover, we became close girlfriends, as actresses on location often do. Well, *sometimes* do. I did once hear of two of them who liked each other. And Melissa and I surely liked each other, and we laughed and gossiped and hung out together through the three weeks of shooting, and we supported each other in the most painful scenes.

One of the first scenes we shot was of the two of us, totally distraught, coming out of a limo after Edgar's funeral. For some reason it took hours to set up the shot, and I was afraid that Melissa might not be able to handle the emotion when the time finally came to replay this painful moment. But I knew what to do.

"If Daddy were producing this movie," I said, "he would have had this shot in the can hours ago."

And our pride in Edgar's ability made the scene work.

Side by side Melissa and I watched the dailies. My considerations were always the most artistic ones: Did I read that line well? Do my thighs look good? When I finally saw the first rough cut of the entire film, I was deeply moved, but not for what seemed like the obvious reason. Yes, of course it was tough to watch the funeral scene and my arguments with Missy. However, what moved me the most was the pride I felt for Melissa in having gone through a horrendous ordeal with style and becoming an admirable young woman and a damn good actress.

By the time the movie went on the air, Melissa and I were each enmeshed in our own lives, mine in New York and hers in California, but by then we knew that our lives would always be inextricably linked, no matter where we lived.

For a mother and daughter who *don't* lose a man to suicide, things can still be tough. A daughter's teenage years can be a mother's attempt to make contact with a UFO: Unintelligible Female Opponent. But Melissa and I had survived those alien encounters and also an encounter with unthinkable tragedy. And now we were bound to each other not just by love but by friendship too.

Whatever your own goals may be, whether they involve family or work, you can reach them the same way I reached mine:

Never take your eye off those goals.
Let no setback discourage you.
Keep going steadily ahead.
And remember the flight of the
    bumblebee.

19

DON'T WORRY,
BE HAPPY

As painful as your challenges may be, they can teach you about your strengths, about who you are and what you value. Armed with that knowledge, you will reach a point where you will want to drop all grudges.

"Wait a minute, Joan," you're saying. "Weren't you just praising revenge? Did it go out of style in the last twenty minutes?"

Yes, revenge is still sweet, but only within a certain period of time. After too long it goes sour, and planning it can even erode you. After a while you have to let go, just as you have to let go of the good things too: your child's childhood, your tennis serve, your having sex more than once a decade.

The losses of all the people I've loved, from my mother to dear friends like Vincent Price and his wife, Coral Browne, have made me try even harder to let people who are still alive know how much I value them. My mother's death was a poignant reminder to always tell people exactly what they mean to me and to keep my temper in check. Never again will I make the mistake of hanging up the phone angrily on anyone, nor will I let warm feelings go unspoken. At least I do have the comfort of knowing that Edgar died aware that I loved him, despite the tough time we were going through.

The greatest thing I learned from Edgar's suicide is that I am strong and can get through anything. Before he swallowed those pills, Edgar made three tapes: for me, for Melissa, and for Tom Pileggi. Melissa and Tom listened to theirs right away. But I couldn't bear to hear Edgar's voice just then — perhaps just never.

The weekend of her college graduation, Melissa said, "Mom, have you heard the tape yet?"

"The new Billy Joel?" I replied.

"You know the one."

"Honey, I just haven't been able to."

"I think it would help you," said a daughter giving wisdom to her mother.

And so, I had my secretary send the tape to Philadelphia. And there, not far from the room where Edgar had killed himself, I listened to something that pierced my heart. In a voice full of love, Edgar said, "I know what I'm doing, Joan. I'm sorry, but I have to do it."

At the end of the tape, he said, "I know you'll get through this, Joan, because you're strong. I know you'll be just fine."

When taping those words, Edgar had known me better than I knew myself. How I wish he had chosen some other way to let me prove my strength, but prove it I did. And you can too: We are all much stronger than we think. One night when I was laughing with friends, I suddenly realized that every one of us had taken blows that we'd thought would finish us; and yet all of us had not only survived but were laughing now. The human spirit is like one of those trick birthday candles: It simply cannot be extinguished.

In life the only thing that you can expect is the unexpected; the only surprise is a day that has none. I am always amused by those annual planners like Filofaxes, in which people delude themselves into thinking that they are controlling the future. Only one entry will always be right:

To be knocked on my butt and get up.

In the years since Edgar's death, I have rebuilt a life for myself full of challenge and purpose. Although I still miss him deeply and am grateful for the time we had together, the love we shared, and the daughter we raised, I am truly happy again.

Man is the only animal that has the power to laugh. In fact, I have always felt that the luckiest people are those described by a writer named Rafael Sabatini, who said of the hero of his novel *Scaramouche* that he was "born with the gift of laughter and the sense that the world was mad."

Of *course* the world is mad! The healthier the economy is, the more the stock market goes down. Sonny Bono is in Congress. And in central New Jersey, there is a sign on the I-95 that says the highway you are on is

95 NORTH
295 SOUTH

In other words you're coming and going at the same time. Perhaps this kind of geography explains why a FedEx package sent from Brooklyn to the Bronx first goes through Nashville, Tennessee. And if you follow I-95 either east or west from Nashville, you will reach Anaheim, Azuza, and Cucamonga. Meanwhile, in the words of the learned Lawrence Peter Berra, "When you reach a fork in the road, take it."

I have been through so much madness that Yogi Berra makes sense to me. And I will raise my demure little voice to tell you: With laughter and courage, you can survive anything and bounce back — and I mean *anything.* Just be honest with yourself about what you have lost, what you want from life, and how you're changing. Seek help when you need it and comfort when you want it. Don't judge yourself too harshly, and don't let anyone *else's* judgment stand in your way.

"Listen to me, sweetheart," Galileo's mother probably told him. "You've got to stop saying that the earth revolves around the sun; it's embarrassing the family. Maybe astronomy just isn't your field. You know, your uncle has a shoe store in Florence."

Above all, like Galileo and Churchill and Dr. Seuss, remember that nothing is impossible and that there *are* happy endings not manufactured by Disney.

To commemorate one such ending, when Melissa graduated from college, I embroidered a needlepoint pillow for our library as a gift to us both for surviving and being able to find happiness again. The pillow said:

WELCOME TO JOAN AND MELISSA'S
EXCELLENT ADVENTURE

And so I wish you luck. More than that, I wish you the vision to create your *own* luck. Branch Rickey, the great general manager who brought Jackie Robinson into baseball, once said, "Luck is the residue of design." In the design of your new life, may you be Frank Lloyd Wright.

And remember: Everyone has a right to be happy, even Princess Diana.

B   26.95
Rive   Thorndike
Rivers   LARGE PRINT
Bouncing Back: I've Survived
Everything . . .

DATE DUE		
JUL 07 1997	FEB 26 1998	
JUL 21 1997		
SEP 08 1997	JUL 20 1999	
SEP 08 1997	JAN 08 2003	
OCT 03 1997		
OCT 20 1997		
NOV 25 1997		
DEC 23 1997		
DEC 29 1997